Contracting for Development

Contracting for Development

The Role of For-Profit Contractors in U.S. Foreign Development Assistance

Rubén Berríos

Westport, Connecticut
London

Library of Congress Cataloging-in-Publication Data

Berríos, Rubén, 1950–
    Contracting for development : the role of for-profit contractors
in U.S. foreign development assistance / Rubén Berríos.
        p.   cm.
    Includes bibliographical references and index.
    ISBN 0–275–96633–X (alk. paper)
    1. United States. Agency for International Development.
    2. Technical assistance, American.   3. Public contracts—United
States.   4. Government purchasing—United States.   I. Title.
    HC60.B432   2000
    338.91'73—dc21   99–34114

British Library Cataloguing in Publication Data is available.

Library of Congress Catalog Card Number: 99–34114
ISBN: 0–275–96633–X

First published in 2000

Praeger Publishers, 88 Post Road West, Westport, CT 06881
An imprint of Greenwood Publishing Group, Inc.
www.praeger.com

Printed in the United States of America

The paper used in this book complies with the
Permanent Paper Standard issued by the National
Information Standards Organization (Z39.48–1984).

10 9 8 7 6 5 4 3 2 1

To Saúl & Saskia

Contents

Contents

Illustrations

Preface

Concern in the rich northern industrialized countries to assist in the alleviation of poverty in the southern less developed countries (LDCs) has been a central impetus behind development aid. Over the last four decades, however, a development industry that has often been more self-serving than caring has arisen. Bilateral aid agencies in the North frequently have focused their attention on some of the symptoms of the failure of development rather than on providing a cure. Further, they have increasingly viewed aid as a profit-making tool rather than as an instrument of assistance. As Korten (1990) puts it, development has become a big business, preoccupied more with its own growth and imperatives than with the people it was originally created to serve (ix).

This book grows out of my concern over the fact that typically only a few cents of every dollar of aid ends in the developing South. The issues discussed here, and my conclusions, will be controversial in the eyes of some government officials and of many in the aid industry. But having studied and worked on development issues for nearly two decades, I have become increasingly convinced that development aid has taken a wrong turn. Much of the development literature has been overly concerned with the effects of aid on the recipient countries. That is, that aid is often wasted because of poor institutional development, corruption, or bureaucratic failures that impede growth. The literature ignores the increasing reliance of bilateral agencies on for-profit contractors who are often the main beneficiaries of aid.

The focus of attention here is government contracting, or more specifically, how USAID awards contracts for development work in LDCs. Despite the good intentions of many in the aid industry, the agency and its staff have become more preoccupied with subsidizing contractors than with the significant issues of development that the southern LDCs face.

Acknowledgments

I am grateful to Phyllis Coontz, Josephine Olson, Louis Picard, and Robert Norman for reading and commenting on an earlier draft. I also wish to thank Rajen Mookerjee, Larry Nowels, Dan Guttman, and James Hecht for their comments on individual chapters. I also want to express a word of gratitude to Marcus Stevenson, director of procurement at USAID, for providing me access to the closed-out contracts and a space to work at the agency during my stay in Washington, D.C. I am particularly grateful to Joseph Beausoleil, my principal contact at USAID, for his support in providing much of the information I requested and for his advice and guidance. Finally, my greatest debt is to my wife, Lillian Thomas, with whom I tested my ideas throughout the entire undertaking. She also read my work with critical rigor and proofread much of the manuscript. Without her encouragement and support, this research would not have taken fruition and materialized in its final form. Nelson Caro and Louis Nosce provided valuable technical support. Jean and Clarke Thomas provided much affection and support. The book is dedicated to my children, who put up with my absences and offered me inspiration. The views expressed and the substantive arguments put forth in these pages are mine alone.

Introduction

In 1993, the Clinton administration announced the National Performance Review, billed as a campaign to "reinvent government." Vice President Al Gore headed the effort and selected a number of departments and agencies to spearhead it. The initiative was billed as a program to streamline government, make it better, more efficient, and more businesslike. The United States Agency for International Development (USAID) was designated as a reinvention laboratory, with the goal of reforming the procurement process and improving the agency's management of development assistance (Gore 1993). The goal was not just to restructure and "do more with less" but to achieve measurable results. It was also a continuation of efforts to make USAID—long the whipping boy of critics who vilified it as a source of handouts to less developed countries (LDCs)—more attractive to Congress by casting the agency as a source of trade promotion and jobs at home. A major strategy was to make privatization (using private providers for public services) more effective. By contracting out its development programs and projects to private for-profit firms as well as to large nonprofit organizations or non-governmental organizations (NGOs), the reasoning went, USAID would become more efficient and businesslike, save money, and provide jobs and income to domestic firms.[1]

Five years later, contracting has moved to a dominant role in USAID's operations. But even though half of USAID funds for development assistance are now channeled in the form of contracts (the other half is in grants), the goals of efficiency, streamlining, and strategies that mirror those of successful businesses are not being achieved. The contracting process is flawed in a number of ways:

- Though often seen as an agency that puts money into foreign hands, USAID is actually a source of contracting dollars and jobs for U.S. companies and organizations. By funding principally U.S. for-profit contractors who in turn deposit their checks in U.S. banks, USAID makes these contractors the main beneficiaries of development assistance.

- Most of the development dollars are awarded in the form of large contracts to a relatively small number of contractors. These large contractors have become a powerful interest group that is able to influence development policy. They are part of the aid lobby, which has some influential contacts and a say in the way policy is shaped.

- Decisions on which countries receive aid and what kinds of aid programs are employed are based on many factors, and the basic questions of what countries are most in need of aid and what kinds of aid are most beneficial often are less important in decision making than questions about what is best for U.S. strategic and political interests, what will best serve the domestic economy and international trade interests, and what types of programs will allow the agency to maintain the political support it needs to survive.

- There is little analysis of whether the results of the contract are beneficial to the recipient country in the long run. The emphasis is on fulfilling the contract, but not necessarily on fulfilling needs. For instance, many of the contracts to assist in the privatization effort in Eastern Europe and the former Soviet Union were poorly managed by firms with little expertise in moving countries to market. Furthermore, these firms worked with little oversight from USAID.

- The procurement process is often neither open nor competitive— large firms that have already done business with the agency have a distinct advantage. Contracts are often awarded following a negotiating process, rather than a bidding process.

- USAID continues to award, for the most part, the types of contracts that are *least* favorable to the agency. Rather than agreeing to incentive-driven-type contracts that reward contractors for efficiency and good results, USAID consistently awards cost-reimbursement or cost-plus fixed-fee—agreeing to a fixed fee plus covering cost overruns incurred by contractors.

- Even in this bare bones fulfillment of a contract, agency expectations are extremely low. Essentially, contractors need only achieve a minimum acceptable performance (the equivalent of a C on a report card) to be eligible to obtain more contracts in the future. Furthermore, many poor performers are permitted to renegotiate their grade evaluations. After reading the agency's evaluation of their performance, they make their rebuttal and are frequently granted the minimum passing performance grade.

The core of this study is an examination of the types of contracts awarded by USAID. The goal is to examine how well the agency is doing in reinventing itself. Does it behave like a private enterprise? How well do contractors perform? How is this experiment in privatization going? USAID has been selected for this analysis because policy makers seeking to transform government have single it out as a test case. Contracting at a single agency committed to a policy of "reinventing government" will serve as a microcosm to examine this aspect of the drive to privatization in government.

Privatization has become the cornerstone of almost all government economic reform packages. When U.S. policy makers seek cost reductions, increased efficiency, and more effective program implementations, they increasingly turn to privatization as a tool.

In its broadest meaning, privatization refers to restrictions on the government's role and to policies that seek to increase the role of market forces in the economy.[2] In the United States, privatization refers mainly to the government's contracting out of public services to private providers. The government purchases the expertise of private firms to provide services that had been performed exclusively by the public sector. The goal of contracting out is to create a more efficient and effective delivery of services through a system that fosters and creates competition, provides better management than public management does, and helps to reduce the size of government. As is always the case with attempts at transforming a large public bureaucracy, making privatization work is challenging.

This study reviews the delivery of development assistance by USAID through contracts, mainly via private for-profit contractors. It focuses on the contracting process at USAID as a way of explaining the transition process toward government privatization. Although U.S. development aid has been channeled in the form of grants as well as contracts, the agency has favored contracts as the principal means of project and program implementation. Although most NGOs and nonprofit organizations receive mainly grants, there are pressures on many of them to enter into contractual arrangements (Robinson 1997).

This study examines USAID's procurement practices—how the agency goes about awarding contracts, who gets them, and how contractors perform—because it is clearly important to how the rest of the process will function. This study asks, essentially, whether USAID is behaving in a genuinely entrepreneurial fashion when awarding contracts. And it examines whether the reinvention of the agency is focused on the presumed goal of a foreign aid agency—promoting successful development in LDCs—or instead on a new mission—providing income and employment for private for-profit firms.

To analyze the procurement process at USAID, a model drawn from economic theory of contracting is used. This model was developed by McAfee and McMillan (1988) and describes three types of contracts: fixed-price, cost-plus, and incentive. The model argues that incentive-type contracts—those that reward contractors for cost savings and/or good performance—are usually the most desirable from the government's point of view when it contracts for services. Fixed-price type contracts are best for the procurement of goods, whereas cost-plus (or cost-reimbursement) contracts are the least desirable. The model further explains how the government can achieve the optimal contract, that is, how it can act like a competitive business, both in how it manages the procurement process and in how it awards contracts.

The study analyzes completed (closed-out) USAID contracts to examine the types of contracts the agency is awarding and whether these are optimal contracts that are consistent with the tenets of privatization and with the "reinvention of government" effort. It uses USAID's past performance evaluations as a way to determine whether the agency is getting the *best value*[3] and to see whether the procurement process is generating positive outcomes.

The study is significant because little is known empirically about contracting for development.

The study documents the practices of private sector contractors, how they compete for USAID contracts, and how they fit into the stated aims and needs of the agency. Ruttan (1996) has noted that foreign aid continues to be one of the least understood aspects of U.S. foreign affairs, which is why this study intends to provide a more informed analysis of contracting for delivering foreign assistance. The research also aims to provide a better understanding of the complexities of a significant and growing consulting market in development and how these firms do business with the government.

Two questions drive the study and are used to examine the analysis and results: (1) Do USAID contracts reflect the principles and practices cited by those who promote contracting? (2) How is USAID doing in terms of its own standards and goals? In addition, the question of whether the reinvented goals of USAID are appropriate will be addressed. Are USAID practices economically sound? Are agency practices likely to help or hinder long-term development policy goals?

NOTES

1. Contracting out is a form of privatization. Although USAID has been a contractor operation since it began in 1961, initially it was contracting academics affiliated with universities and nonprofit entities. It has been during the past fifteen years that the agency has become a source of contracting dollars for for-profit consulting firms.

2. In LDCs and the former socialist countries of Central and Eastern Europe, privatization often refers to the sale of assets of state-owned enterprises. This has also been called "denationalization." Aktan (1995) and Seidenstat (1996) call this only one form of privatization. Another form of privatization is load shedding, by which the public sector or voluntary organizations can pick up the slack. Another form is franchising, which is when the government gives exclusive rights to a private firm to produce and supply some part of a particular service.

3. According to the Federal Acquisition Regulation (FAR, Part 15, Section 2.101), *best value* means the expected outcome of an acquisition that, in the government's estimation, provides the greatest overall benefit in response to the requirement. This means that the agency considers one or a combination of source selection approaches (cost factors and technical capabilities). The relative importance of cost or price may vary depending on whether the requirement is clearly definable and risk is minimal. The less definitive the requirement, the greater the risk, and, therefore the more

technical consideration will play in source selection. See Cibinic and Nash (1998).

1

Development Aid as a Way of Promoting U.S. Self-Interests

Foreign aid is an issue that tends to ignite strong feelings in the United States. Foreign development aid in general and USAID in particular have been fiercely criticized as a waste of money. Senator Jesse Helms (R-N.C.), who has been instrumental in moving USAID closer to the State Department, and has also been a major player in reducing funds for the agency, characterizes foreign aid as "throwing money down foreign rat holes."[1]

The common perception in the press is that foreign aid is unpopular among the public. Many citizens believe too much is spent on foreign aid—until they find out how little money is allocated. Members of the American public have wildly exaggerated notions of what percentage of the budget goes toward foreign aid, and when asked to suggest an appropriate amount, most name a figure that is far greater than current spending. According to a comprehensive study of public attitudes, when given the actual levels of spending, few regard it as too high (Kull, Destler, and Ramsay 1997).

What even fewer people realize is that if indeed the money is being thrown down rat holes, those holes are in the United States, not foreign countries. USAID has become a conduit for funds that are largely channeled into U.S. private contracting firms and non-governmental organizations.

The fact is that the agency works mainly with a network of well-established for-profit contractors, providing them a business lifeline. According to Nowels and Tarnoff (1997), "most foreign aid money is spent to procure U.S. goods and services. By law, nearly all U.S. assistance must be spent on American produced items, although waivers are permitted under certain circumstances. The agency procurement in FY1996 totaled about $3.2 billion. USAID estimates that goods and services from U.S. sources represented about $2.6 billion, or 83 percent of all procurement" (10-11). Another report also notes that "80 percent of the total foreign assistance budget goes for goods and services that the U.S. Government buys from business all across America. In 1994, more than $10 billion in foreign assistance was spent on American products and services. This supports about 200,000 U.S. jobs" (Business Alliance for International Economic Development 1996, 2-3).[2]

To understand how this has happened, it is necessary to examine the history of U.S. development aid and USAID, and to understand the political-economic environments in which the agency evolved and in which it now functions.

U.S. foreign development assistance began formally a half-century ago. The political and economic environment in which it developed was obviously profoundly different from that which exists today. A description of foreign aid and a discussion of the historical background is important, because it shows how radical a change the policy shifts that began in the 1980s represented for USAID.

THE EVOLUTION OF U.S. POST-WORLD WAR II FOREIGN AID

Foreign aid emerged as an institutionalized policy of the United States government after World War II when its goals were articulated by President Harry Truman. It began formally with the European Recovery Program, better known as the Marshall Plan, a program designed to assist in the rehabilitation of postwar Europe. The focus shifted to the developing world with President Truman's Four Point Program. The recipients of the Marshall Plan aid signed the convention establishing the Organization for European Economic Cooperation in 1948. In 1961, the Organization for Economic Cooperation and Development (OECD) was created and accepted the United States as full member, leading to its increased role in providing economic and development assistance to less developed countries (LDCs).

Assistance to developing countries by the United States was not something new. Government agencies and philanthropic organizations had organized a broad range of technical assistance, aid programs, loans and gifts in agriculture, health, education, and financial reform. Some of these programs began in the nineteenth century and then grew in scope as the United States became increasingly wealthy and powerful (Curti and Birr 1954; White 1994; Brown et al. 1953). There had been some assistance provided to Latin America before and during World War II, and assistance to Turkey, Greece, China, and other East Asian countries immediately after the war (Ruttan 1996). However, these programs were not a part of the official U.S. foreign policy. They were a collection of public and private efforts, arising from different needs and motivations. It was not until the latter part of the 1940s that a coherent policy took shape.

The emergence of the modern foreign aid policy era, better known as Official Development Assistance (ODA), stipulated that the funds transferred be used for purposes of economic development.[3] Griffin (1991) notes that as a post–World War II phenomenon, "foreign aid programmes originated as part of the ideological confrontation known as the Cold War" and the motives behind it were always more political than economic.

The commitment to foreign assistance beyond the Marshall Plan can be traced to President Truman's inaugural address in 1949. The Four Point Program outlined in this speech marked a shift in the focus of American foreign aid from post-war reconstruction to economic development (Pastor 1980; Ruttan 1996). This represented a decisive break with tradition because, with few exceptions, "previous aid [policy] had not focused on development as an issue" (Ruttan 1996, 49). The Four Point Program resulted in the Act for International Development of 1950.

The early aid regime had a distinctly Eurocentric character because much of the aid in fact went to Europe. However, this shifted in the early 1950s with the U.S. government's concern over the Chinese revolution. The Korean War further influenced development strategies. Throughout the 1950s, the security objective of U.S. foreign aid was much more evident than its humanitarian or economic development objectives. Development assistance served mainly as a functional extension of the ideological confrontation between East and West. As a result of the perceived threat of communism to U.S. national security, foreign assistance was to be used as a counterbalance measure to address that threat. The geographical emphasis was still Europe (mainly Greece and Turkey), but at this time it shifted to include the Asia/Pacific region (Taiwan, Korea). As a major provider of economic aid, the United States granted this aid to reward allies and withheld it to punish enemies.

The U.S. Agency for International Development (USAID) was created in 1961 under the Foreign Assistance Act, and became the government agency to dispense bilateral assistance abroad. The Kennedy Administration essentially separated economic from military aid and consolidated economic aid and technical programs into USAID. Furthermore, it changed geographical direction, placing the focus on LDCs. Under Kennedy, appropriations for foreign aid programs increased rapidly, largely to counter expanded Soviet aid to a number of countries in the Third World (Hough 1986). In the early 1960s, foreign aid become a vital tool to further the foreign policy goals of the United States. It was the time of the launching of the Peace Corps and the Alliance for Progress, a cooperative program designed to promote development in Latin America (Rabe 1988). When the Development Assistance Committee (DAC) was formed in the early sixties, the United States accounted for just under half of the world's aid. By then, other countries such as the United Kingdom, France, the Netherlands, and Belgium had recovered from the effects of the war and had also begun to provide a greater share of aid, particularly to their former colonies.

The 1960s was a period of decolonization, amid geopolitical tensions, but now aid lost much of its appeal except as an instrument in the global fight against communism. Developing countries began using the United Nations as a forum for articulating their collective needs. At a 1968 United Nations Commission on Trade and Development (UNCTAD) meeting, donor states announced that they would provide 0.7 percent of their GNP for development assistance. This and other long-term goals were outlined in the Pearson Report.[4] The United States never accepted the target of 0.7 percent of GNP laid down by the Pearson Report, but since it had the largest economy, its contribution was actually greater in volume than that of any other donor. The importance of U.S. foreign assistance, however, depended on the particular administration that was in office and the political environment at the time (Morrison and Purcell 1988).

In its early years, USAID focused primarily on large-scale improvement projects (e.g., road construction, irrigation). During its first decades of existence there were few contracts, and they were awarded mostly to experts affiliated with academic institutions. The agency had a decentralized structure and an incentive to spend its annual allocation, rather than try to hold costs down, to continue receiving that level of funding. In an era when aid was seen as a way to counter the influence of political rivals of the United States, a greater emphasis was placed on a broad presence of programs than on the performance of individual projects and programs.

This focus shifted in 1973 when USAID implemented a number of programs and administrative reforms that emphasized a basic human needs approach to development (Ruttan 1996). These new guidelines, known as "New Directions," targeted the poor segments of the population in developing countries and encouraged employment generation and more equitable income distribution within LDCs. In light of this concern, agriculture, rural development, health, nutrition, and family planning were emphasized in development assistance budgets. This approach to development also linked human rights and foreign aid, making respect for human rights on the part of the aid-recipient country a professed political objective (Moon 1991).

In 1981, following the election of Ronald Reagan as president, his administration reasserted the primacy of Cold War issues and proposed yet another change in direction at USAID (Lebovic 1988; Sewell and Contee 1991). Now the overriding concern was Soviet influence, which was considered to be the source of unrest in the Third World. As development assistance goals faded into the background, security-oriented economic aid became the preferred form of aid. Although aid grew, the increase was very uneven. Security-related assistance grew from 55 percent to 67 percent from 1981 to 1985, as the share going to development assistance decreased from 45 percent to 33 percent. According to Sewell and Contee (1991), security-related assistance made up 72 percent of total U.S. aid in FY1988.

The Reagan administration also wanted to streamline USAID, because of greater concern with costs, and change its goals, moving away from what was termed a basic human needs orientation to the promotion of private sector activities. This shift created new pressures, because business goals often conflicted with development goals. On the one hand, USAID maintained the basic needs rhetoric, but on the other, it increased funding for only one such program: health care. Programs such as agriculture, education, population, and human resources were de-emphasized.[5] Central to this new approach was the Private Enterprise Initiative launched by the Reagan administration in 1981 and supplemented in 1990 by the Partnership for Business Development Initiative (Berger 1985; CRS 1989; Ruttan 1996). The goal of this new initiative was to encourage private sector involvement.

The initiative had three components: (1) utilization of the private sector as a delivery mechanism, that is, greater reliance on the private rather than on the public sector; (2) expansion of private enterprise development by encouraging LDCs to open their economies to greater reliance on competitive markets and private enterprise; (3) implementation of policy reform by encouraging LDC governments to promote free market principles. This last policy guideline, enforced during the past fifteen years, has made an increasing amount of aid conditional on the implementation by LDCs of structural adjustment policies (Berg 1991; Nelson 1990; Stokke 1996; White 1994). Conditionality was accentuated by the debt crisis that emerged in the 1980s, but now covers other issues of policy reform as well.

As a result, much of USAID project and non-project aid to LDCs began to have a private enterprise element to it and sought to use the private sector to carry out USAID's traditional social service activities (Congressional Research Service 1989). The change was based on the belief that private enterprise is the best engine for promoting development and stimulating growth. In an effort to redefine its role, USAID took the lead, along with multilateral financial institutions, in promoting the divestiture of public enterprises, privatization, and the transfer of public funding from government to the private sector.

USAID focused not only on advancing private enterprise abroad but also on nurturing it at home, by actively encouraging U.S. private firms to become USAID contractors (GAO 1992c; GAO 1992d). The practice of contracting out had always included private American concerns as well as those of non-governmental organizations (NGOs) and universities. But with the Partnership for Business Development Initiative launched in 1990, the agency began to specifically target private U.S. firms and to publicize policy changes made to encourage greater U.S. private sector involvement (GAO 1992d; OECD 1995a; Ruttan 1996).

As a result, private contractors have become an important source of power and are in fact the main agents influencing the course of present-day development assistance (USAID 1995b). As a 1995b OECD study reaffirms, the shift by USAID was intended primarily to promote a climate conducive to private sector development (e.g., financial market development, trade and investment promotion, privatization). USAID could then attempt to deflect criticism that it was pouring money needed at home into foreign countries by asserting that a high percentage of its funds actually stayed in the United States.

USAID's decision to contract out was partly spurred by concerns about cost containment and economic efficiency (Ruttan 1996; CRS 1991; Rondinelli 1989; Zimmerman and Hook 1996), but was also politically inspired. USAID became part of the new wave of privatization that was to attract the support of contractors and other private businesses. Criticized for its poor management of development aid programs, USAID turned to contracting out as a way to ensure that assistance resources would benefit, above all, U.S. economic interests.

FOREIGN AID IN THE POST-COLD WAR ERA

With the end of the Cold War, U.S. foreign assistance programs have been undergoing a reassessment as the scope and complexity of aid relations have increased in the 1990s. The changes are occurring in the conditionality focus and in the regional and country priority allocations of aid. Foreign aid has not been popular in Congress, and actual financial support for it in the 1990s has reached its lowest point (O'Hanlon and Graham 1997).[6] There are several reasons for this. First, lawmakers have been hostile to programs that do not appear to directly benefit the domestic economy. Second, the conclusion of the Cold War removed strategic rationales for aid giving. Third, public and congressional opposition to foreign assistance has been heightened by the misuse of U.S. foreign assistance either on ineffective programs or in some corrupt and repressive governments having little to show for economic development.

Moreover, the agency administering foreign aid "has been viewed by many observers as incompetent, poorly managed, and demoralized" (Tarnoff and Nowels 1994, 2). Finally, preoccupation with domestic issues has increased, and signs of "aid fatigue" have surfaced. Government audits have also reported that the foreign aid delivery system is complex, costly, and has failed to achieve its mission (GAO 1993). As a result, foreign aid budgets have witnessed a steady decline during the past ten years (O'Hanlon and Graham 1997; Congressional Budget Office 1997).

In the mid-1990s, foreign aid was among the least popular spending programs of the federal government (Epstein, Nowels, and Hildreth 1998) In 1997, U.S. spending on foreign affairs, according to the Congressional Budget Office (1997), reached its lowest level, falling to less than 1 percent. "Although other major categories of federal spending have increased over the past 10 years, foreign aid outlays fell by 32 percent between 1985 and 1995. Overall federal spending rose almost 15 percent" (CBO 1997, 10). As Figure 1.1 shows, by 1995, U.S. foreign aid as a percentage of GNP was at its lowest since 1950.

During the mid-1990s, the Clinton Administration shifted its approach from a proactive attempt to reform development assistance to protecting it from further budget cuts pushed by conservatives in Congress. Some influential conservative. members of Congress, such as Senator Jesse Helms (chairman of the Foreign Relations Committee), sought to dissolve USAID, arguing that foreign development aid was a waste of taxpayers' money. To prevent this from happening, the administration agreed to make USAID accountable to the State Department. Although this allowed USAID to remain in business, it could sharply curtail its independence, and "in practice may ensure greater State Department control over aid programs" (Haugaard 1997, 30). Now USAID's administrator reports exclusively to the secretary of state rather than the president, and AID's budget must pass through the State Department.

Under the Clinton administration, USAID underwent some restructuring of its bureaucracy, in accordance with its new approach of doing more with less. However, the agency has also downplayed new strategies for addressing poverty in favor of promoting markets. Providing aid to the private sector and strengthening a business climate have played a more active role in develop-

Figure 1.1
U.S. Foreign Aid as a Percentage of GNP

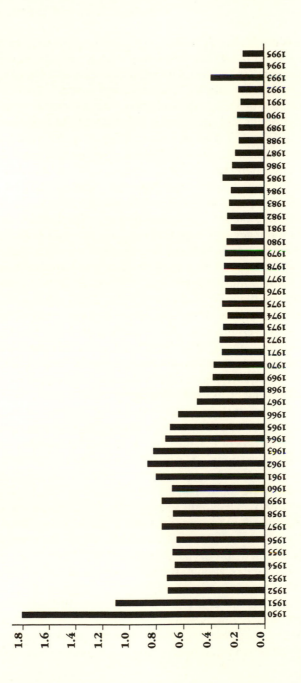

Source: USAID, *U.S. Overseas Loans and Grants and Assistance from International Organizations,* 1995, 1996; IMF, *International Financial Statistics,* various years

ment assistance in the 1990s. Even social programs intended to ameliorate hardship are frequently tied to structural adjustment requirements. In this sense, the Clinton administration's aid policy has been a reaffirmation of the neoliberal model.

With the demise of the Cold War, foreign assistance as a way of winning friends and allies abroad in practice has come to play a secondary role in U.S. foreign policy. The policy that now prevails is privatization and the push for free markets and free trade. There are hardly any competing development models or "socialist" alternatives left in the so-called Third World to justify to Congress increases in aid. Recipients of aid must demonstrate that they are free market reformers and are committed to a new liberal order that stresses the supremacy of the market over the state. In some sense, foreign aid is still a reward to U.S. allies, and the main condition for receiving aid is to show allegiance and commitment to further economic liberalization. For instance, during the 1980s, Nicaragua was punished swiftly for its socialist policies. This included the suspension of aid, as well as the arming of the Contras trying to topple the Sandinista government, and the rewarding with increased aid of the neighboring countries (Honduras and Costa Rica) that were willing to harbor Contra camps and training facilities.

An important feature of U.S. foreign policy in the 1990s has been a movement toward disengagement in world affairs. This is particularly evident in lower budgets for international spending, reduction of U.S. diplomatic presence in the developing world, and mounting arrears of U.S. dues to the United Nations and other multilateral organizations. For instance, a recent study notes that the perception of U.S. foreign policy practitioners is that the American public has little interest in international issues (Kull, Destler, and Ramsay 1997). But careful analysis reveals that there is a great deal of support for engagement and that the United States should play an active role in international affairs (Kull 1995). The perception is that "most Americans dislike foreign aid," when in fact, most believe the United States should provide a larger share in helping the world's poor.

As part of the effort to restructure USAID and downsize its overseas presence, between FY1994 and FY1998, twenty nine missions were closed, more than half of them in Africa. According to the official version, "the overall rationale for this was to achieve better results by focusing shrinking resources on those countries where development results could be expected" (DAC 1998, 27). Meanwhile in Washington, staff levels have sustained a 22 percent cut during the same period.

As the millennium comes to a close, some of the important issues in the coming century are the environment, population, drug trafficking, immigration, and terrorism. These are issues that foreign aid addresses and that are vital to American interests, defined in the most narrow way possible. Although the American public remains misinformed about foreign development assistance, the overwhelming majority embrace the principle of giving foreign aid to countries in need (Kull 1995; Manzur and Sechler 1997). Most people endorse the importance of solving problems at home, but only 8 percent wanted to do away with foreign aid.

TYPES AND OBJECTIVES OF FOREIGN AID

Foreign aid takes many forms, and the nature and magnitude of its effects have been a subject of considerable debate and controversy. Aid can be a catalyst for change, but more often than not it is only one of many factors that determine development outcomes. Foreign aid is often seen quite differently by the donor and by the recipient countries. Although economic development is often the stated goal of donors, there are many different objectives that can drive foreign assistance programs. These can sometimes bear very little relation to actual need as manifested by hunger or poverty.

Foreign aid is provided bilaterally or multilaterally by donor governments and organizations in the developed northern countries to the southern developing countries. Foreign assistance has not been a single unified program, but rather, a complex instrument of national and foreign policy.

Foreign aid can take the form of direct transfer of funds, soft loans (with 25 percent grant element), in-kind (e.g., food aid), and, of course, technical assistance. Foreign aid also encompasses economic assistance (balance of payments support and debt relief), military assistance, and export credits. Often private funds from voluntary agencies are also included. This study considers only development assistance that is channeled through USAID contracts. Export credits and grants do not involve contracts. Military assis-

tance does, but is guided by a very different set of concerns—
alliances, treaties, national security—from those that drive development aid.

USAID's budget represents less than one-half of one percent of
the federal budget. Of the foreign aid budget, USAID is responsible
for only 65 percent of the funds, although only about one half of it
is actually controlled by the agency. Aid provided through USAID
falls under three categories: Economic Support Fund (ESF),
Development Assistance, and Food for Peace (food aid). The remainder of U.S. foreign aid is handled by the executive branch (the
Treasury Department through multilateral banks, the State
Department through multilateral institutions such as the World
Bank, United Nations, and Department of Defense). Smaller
resources are also allocated to such organizations as the Peace
Corps and the Inter-American Foundation.

One of the most important categories, which makes up more
than half of U.S. economic assistance, is the ESF. This fund is
designed to assist political allies who experience balance of payments problems. It is also a cash transfer for commodity imports
from the donor, or it is used for specific development projects.
Although technically it is a form of economic aid, ESF also functions
as a type of military assistance. According to Hoy (1998), "the diplomatic importance of ESF resources is evident by the fact that the
State Department, not USAID, plays the primary role in allocating
them, as is listed in the foreign aid appropriations bill as security
assistance" (18). Nearly 85 percent of the ESF budget is earmarked
for Israel and Egypt. Most recently, the new programs designed for
the Central and Eastern European countries, including the newly
independent states (NIS) of the former Soviet Union, received in
FY1999 $1.3 billion.

The other important category is development assistance, which
is provided in the form of grants and contracts. Nearly half of the
money that is allocated by USAID is actually awarded as contracts,
in the form of project assistance or non-project program aid. Both
could involve technical assistance to provide needed expertise for
a specific investment, or for a program, or for help in building devel-
opment-related institutions. Most of the contracts are awarded to
private for-profit contractors. The rest of the money goes to non-
governmental organizations (NGOs) and private voluntary organi-

zations (PVOs) to do work in specific sectors, such as health, education, population control, and rural development. Although between 1962 and 1988, loans represented 32 percent of total military and economic assistance, these have substantially decreased because of the indebtness of many LDCs. By the end of the 1990s, loans represented less than 2 percent of total aid appropriations.

Although foreign development assistance is administered through bilateral, multilateral, and private organizations, this study focuses on the first, specifically assistance provided by the U.S. government. The bulk of foreign aid comes from bilateral assistance. There is a preference of bilateral aid over multilateral aid resulting from, among other factors, fear of losing control over the use of aid, and a desire to guard the benefits that accrue to the donor from a direct control of the use of aid.

The motives for foreign assistance fall into three broad categories: *humanitarian* (moral and ethical), *political* (strategic), and *economic* (commercial) self-interest grounds. The humanitarian argument relates to past injustices, uneven distribution of global resources, and a moral obligation to help the least-developed (Lumsdaine 1993; Ruttan 1989). The political self-interest argument is based on the notion that aid will strengthen the political commitment of the recipient to the donor. Since foreign aid is often utilized as a tool of foreign policy by a donor country, the allocation patterns of aid often reflect national self-interests. In the case of the United States, strategic political considerations have been a major motivation for aid (Conteh-Morgan 1990; Hook 1995; Porter 1990; Zimmerman 1993). For example, a key political issue during the Cold War was the containment of Soviet influence in what was known as the Third World. In the words of Baldwin (1985), "One of the most—if not *the* most—important objectives of postwar American foreign policy, including American foreign aid programs, has been to limit the expansion of communism" (326).

The argument that development assistance serves a donor country's economic self-interest is based on the premise that aid promotes exports and generates employment in the donor country. Arguments promoting commercial objectives are frequently made not only through official and political pronouncements, but also by commercial interests seeking to elicit support for foreign aid programs (Business Alliance 1996). For instance, food aid can initiate commercial contacts to increase agricultural exports. Much foreign assistance is tied to the purchase of goods such as food or equipment from the donor country. These purchases directly benefit the producers in these countries.

Donor countries often pursue their own commercial interests through their aid programs. For example, there exists a practice often referred to as aid tying. This is a requirement that some portion of purchases of equipment or of goods under aid-financed projects be procured from suppliers in the donor country. This practice can reduce the developmental effectiveness and the value of aid, because the donor is not always the least-cost supplier of goods (Hewitt and Killick 1996; Jepma 1991, 1994). Aid that emphasizes infrastructure projects rather than social programs, have a greater chance of supporting country exports. Furthermore, the pursuit of a donor's developmental and commercial goals tends to bias the allocation of aid away from the poorest countries toward the middle-income countries and in favor of more capital-intensive projects. These policies in the end can sometimes reduce the quality of development assistance and the effectiveness of the aid in promoting economic development (Development Committee 1986).

In the case of the United States, the beneficial role foreign aid can play in the domestic economy is often cited as the reason for supporting aid programs. In a congressional hearing in September 1996, the Subcommittee on Foreign Operations stressed that "foreign assistance programs benefit the U.S. economy by increasing exports and creating jobs" (U.S. Senate 1996). It also emphasized that "our foreign aid helps pave the way for America's private sector. It opens up markets, U.S. trade, and investment." This justification for development assistance implies that foreign aid does not always have to go where the need is greatest, but rather where there is a potential market for U.S. goods.

Since there is a more careful weighing of the political advantage on a country by country basis, bilateral aid increasingly comes with many attached conditions. These conditions can involve economic policy reforms or political changes by the recipient country, or simply a requirement that goods and services procured with aid money be obtained from the donor country.

Aid is often politicized. A case in point is the $1 billion aid package to Panama proposed by former President George Bush after he ordered the invasion to topple dictator Manuel Noriega. Another instance is after the collapse of the communist system in Central and Eastern Europe, when the agenda for Western donors was to secure the demise of Soviet-type economies and to transform these countries quickly by focusing on privatization and remaking them into Western-style capitalist economies. During the first six years of the 1990s, nearly three-fourths of aid was being channeled to privatization and private sector development, reflecting the U.S. government's political desire to quickly restructure the economies of these countries.

Glossy brochures from aid donors portray a particular image of the need for and uses of aid. They emphasize noble motives answering grave need and promise the alleviation of suffering. Hidden is the fact that aid has become a massive enterprise that generates a huge fund-raising machine. Aid organizations that compete with each other for government money and projects do work in Africa and other regions. The organizations have gone to these areas to alleviate the misery, and most say they have an impact on systems that are in disarray. But there is frequently a cynical manipulation of the humanitarian impulses behind aid that keeps the aid establishment going and the aid business machine greased.

Finally, another reason for extending aid is that many LDCs cannot obtain adequate amounts of external capital from private sources because they lack creditworthiness, or because they lack the necessary physical and institutional infrastructure, or because few private investors are willing to invest or lend under such conditions. These are established facts, and clearly some mechanism is needed to get capital flowing into these countries. What is of concern here is the overreaching effect of the aid machine in the name of development and humanitarian assistance.

NOTES

1. The incendiary remarks by Senator Helms were made at a press conference in Raleigh, North Carolina on 9 November, 1994, *Time*, 5 December, 1995, p. 35. It should be made clear that it was the House Republicans in 1995/96 who initiated and sustained most of the budget cuts.

2. The $10 billion figure mentioned here includes military as well as economic aid. There is a difference between the various aid "spigots"

(development aid, ESF, NIS, food, etc). Since ESF especially transfers funds mainly as cash or commodity import programs, procurement source data can be misleading when it is all mixed together.

3. "Aid" or "assistance" refers to financial flows and technical cooperation that qualify as Official Development Assistance (ODA) as defined by the Development Assistance Committee of the Organization for Economic Cooperation and Development (OECD). *Project aid*, according to Hoy (1998), is "assistance provided for specific activities with a predetermined outcome as a goal, such as construction or engineering services." Some examples are infrastructure projects (e.g., road, electricity, pipe water). The final outcome provides concrete evidence of how money was spent. *Program aid* is assistance that goes to particular economic sectors to solve specific problems. The terms and conditions have to be worked out by donor and recipient. Projects are normally designed around programs, which are more broadly defined. Under the Automated Directive System launched by USAID, the term *project* has been eliminated and replaced with *activity*. In USAID, the emphasis has always been on projects or activities that are carried out to impact development.

4. The influential 1969 report was titled *Partners in Development* and was written under the chairmanship of Lester Pearson by the Commission on International Development.

5. Although the Reagan administration pressed for less development aid overall and added the private initiative, security aid also went up. Thus the Reagan Administration presided over one of the fastest rises in foreign aid spending during his first term in office. Health care rose largely because Congress created new accounts for child survival and HIV/AIDs programs, and these came at the expense of agriculture and education (other than basic ed). Pressures to reduce population aid came not because of a BHN de-emphasis, but because of the abortion debate and the "Mexico City" policy of the Reagan White House. There were other forces at work in modifying aid spending allocations, not just those exclusively initiated by USAID.

6. This has been the trend until 1997, even though in 1998 the trend was slightly reversed. For FY1997 Congress actually approved more for development aid than the Administration had actually requested. This was quite a shift from previous years.

2

Contracting Out as a Form of Privatization

To understand how the development assistance system works, it's necessary to understand how contracting works, and how it has come to dominate the way business is done in and outside governments. USAID has become part of a global phenomenon in which private firms are engaged to provide goods and services. This chapter provides an overview of contracting out in order to make the context in which USAID is operating clear.

DEFINING CONTRACTING OUT

Government contracting out can be defined as public financing of private provision. The business equivalent is outsourcing for the services needed to support the government agency's mission. Contracting involves government (or firms) using competitive bidding to determine who should have the opportunity to produce or deliver goods and/or services. The decision to contract out is often based on the assumption that the government can reduce costs by obtaining services from private firms under contract instead of doing the work using federal employees. Contracting out is an alternative to the traditional method of delivering public services by public agencies by transferring its functions to the private sector. It is an explicit attempt to bring the pressure of the marketplace to bear on the provision of government services (Ascher 1989; Roth 1987).

Contracting out has long been used in the private sector. What makes it of interest is that it is now being used in the public sector. In the last fifteen years there has been a significant growth in the

private-market provision of government services on the grounds
that the public sector is not as efficient in allocating resources. An
important aspect in the effort to reform the public sector has been
the privatization of certain government services with the goal of
achieving greater efficiency. Hence, contracting out has been promoted as a mechanism to cure some of the ills of public sector provision.

A number of factors have led to the push to privatize and thus
restrain the growth of government expenditures. These include the
recession of the early 1980s, the growing concern about the federal government's budget deficit, and the political opposition to
increases in tax rates (Savoie 1994). Although the primary aim has
been to cut costs, the thrust toward privatization has also been
motivated by a political philosophy based on the aim of reducing
the role of government in public provision of services. According
to Seidenstad (1996), the growing power of this message was
reflected in the election of Ronald Reagan in 1980 and his reelec-
tion in 1984 (467).

Privatization is an issue that has led to intense debates among
scholars about the role of government in the delivery of service
(Gormley 1991). Advocates of privatization say that the public sector is systematically distorted, inefficient, and bloated (Fitzgerald
1988; Savas 1987). Proponents claim that contracting out is efficient because (1) it drives costs down by fostering competition; (2)
it relieves budgetary pressures; (3) private for-profit firms are better
managed than government agencies in providing the same services;
and (4) it increases the flexibility of government operations. Hence,
underlying the pressure to privatize the public sector in times of
tight budgets is the promise of greater efficiency and lower cost
(Savas 1987; Donahue 1989; Kemp 1991; Lopez-de-Silames et al.
1997).

According to Domberger and Jensen (1997), contracting out
has both and economic and public policy dimensions. The public
policy issue refers to the proper role of the public sector and the
problems of accountability when private firms supply the service.
The economics of contracting refers to how contracting generally
leads to competitive prices (an efficient outcome) but also carries
transaction costs that can offset the benefits.

A public policy concern that has been raised in cases of contracting out is the loss of public sector accountability. This means that once contractors take control of service provision, the issue of accountability becomes blurred, since the contractors are not entirely responsible for the activity, but the agency that is account-able is not directly involved. Other concerns are the difficulties in monitoring the quality of service delivery and the loss of long-term expertise of in-house capability in the government agency.

The economics of contracting stresses that contracting out can yield short-term savings and long-term benefits. First and most important, competition for contracts results in lower costs. However, some observers emphasize that it may not always be more economically efficient. The reasons given are that: (1) contracting out can result in increased costs when factoring in the process of competitive tendering, transaction costs, monitoring costs, and costs of enforcing contracts (Carver 1989; Prager 1992; Williamsom 1979); (2) contracting out may not lead to lower costs if the con-tract does not provide incentives to minimize costs (Domberger and Jensen 1997; Downs and Larkey 1986); (3) contracting out may not be less costly if the bidding process is not as competitive as it is widely believed (Greene 1994; Starr 1987; Prager 1994; Hanrahan 1987); (4) contracting out may not lead to lower costs if the fixed costs of bidding are high, thus favoring large for-profit private con-tractors that may not be the best to manage development projects and shutting out potential bidders (Hecht 1996b; Lecomte 1986).

ECONOMIC LIBERALIZATION, THE MINIMALIST STATE, AND DEVELOPMENT AID

Economic liberalization all over the world that led to micro-economic reform over the last decade and a half has reoriented the way governments provide goods and services. One aspect of reform that has captured the most attention has been the increasing liberalization in economic management leading to the privatization of government services (Ikenberry 1990; Geddes 1995; Meier 1993). Privatization and market liberalization have been a key part of the policy agenda. In public policy discussion, as Starr (1989) notes, privatization refers to the shift of activities or functions from the state to the private sector. At the heart of this reform process, notes King (1994), has been the movement away from unquestioned in-house provision of many services to a reliance on competitive tendering and contracting out to outside providers. This goes from garbage collection to water provision and treatment to development assistance.

The liberalization trend is not an isolated phenomenon. It forms part of a broader ideological shift favoring market-based solutions and emphasizing the importance of competition in economic development (Green 1995). Economists and politicians who support the change point to cases of inefficient functioning of the public sector because of government intervention and see government as a large public monopoly associated with inefficiency, waste, and unresponsiveness. Mitchell and Simmons (1995) stress that the changes taking place are not confined to the less developed countries (LDCs) but are part of a worldwide trend that is using the market as a mechanism to initiate competition and decentralized decision making, and to emphasize individual property rights.

Liberalization, by which is meant a policy shift toward the market, refers to the relaxation of government controls and opening up the economy to competitive pressures. Liberalization policies are compatible with the tenets of economic liberalism: prices and production are to be determined by the free play of market forces, and governments are to confine themselves to the provision of the infrastructure necessary for markets to work effectively. Winston (1993) notes that a key aspect of the liberalization process has been deregulation, which has led to considerable reduction in the size of the state.

In essence, there is a reconceptualization of the role of the state in policy making as a result of growing liberalization. Neoliberalism as a strand of thought in political economy has advanced strong arguments for privatization of public services, and its advocates are the leading proponents of a minimal state.[1] They stress that market forces, private initiatives, and competition would be a way of allocating resources more efficiently (Nelson 1990; McNeil 1981; Krueger et al. 1989; Browne 1990).

The shift away from focusing on the central role of the state in development in favor of private sector development is mostly associated with the economic difficulties many LDCs faced in the 1980s. These problems were exacerbated by the debt crisis. Multilateral financial institutions, such as the International Monetary

Fund and the World Bank, proposed economic reforms based on policies to strengthen market forces. The widespread adoption of a new development paradigm refocusing on the role of a leaner state was heightened by the importance of the private sector in the development effort. Initially, these reforms were emphasized as a way for LDCs to earn their creditworthiness before the international financial sector. As these reforms were put in place in many LDCs, OECD donor countries developed a consensus validating these efforts (OECD 1995a).

Political support for these adjustment policies was drawn from economic elites with the backing of multilateral banks. Similar policies had been tested under bureaucratic-authoritarian regimes of Latin America's southern cone (Chile and Argentina) in the second half of the 1970s. In rebalancing public spending, governments often curtailed social service spending. Private for-profit contractors, non-governmental organizations (NGOs) and private voluntary organizations (PVOs) have picked up some of the services no longer provided by the government. However, as Vellinga (1997) puts it, their contribution to structural solutions to the problems of urban and rural poverty is small (10). Although these policies succeed in restoring investor confidence, the withdrawal of the state from social policy areas has created a dualism of those who participated and those who were excluded from development-led growth. Proponents of tough structural adjustment policies argue that the changes eventually will benefit all sectors of the economy.

Similarly in the United States and other industrialized countries, pressure came from budget deficits, recognition of inefficiencies, and growing conservatism that led to economic liberalism. All this has led to a redefinition of a new role of the state to ensure a more effective government.

THE DEBATE OVER CONTRACTING OUT

Much of the theoretical basis for the advocacy of contracting out comes from public choice theory. Thoroughly grounded in laissez-faire individualism and free-market economics, public choice theorists such as Buchanan (1977) and Tullock (1990) argue that the government should play a limited role in the economy because the competitive marketplace produces goods and services more efficiently and responsibly than the government. Moreover, the public choice school argues that altering the delivery arrangements of public services will slow the pace of government growth. In this sense, contracting out is seen as a cost-cutting measure, a way of downsizing the public sector, and as offering new opportunities for private business.

The arguments of scholars identified with public choice theory and proponents of government downsizing have been influential in convincing politicians to embrace attempts at privatizing government. Using the neoclassical framework, public choice theorists argue that there is greater merit in private as opposed to public sector service provision. According to public choice theory, there is an element of rent seeking in the formulation of government policy, which suggests that there is a tendency for government programs to cause rather than to cure economic inefficiencies (Hanke and Dowdle 1987; Starr 1989). The theory suggests that whatever the market can do well should be left to the market; the government should step in only in case of market failure (e.g., in case of externalities, public goods, or insufficient competition).

The theory of contracting stresses that competition between potential bidders creates incentives to minimize costs, which provides a competitive edge in a market. The claim has been that contracting out is a cost-efficient method that responds quickly to the desires of customers and provides benefits where competition and the market have traditionally been absent. According to King (1994), the potential benefits from contracting out include lower costs, improved service delivery and quality, and greater flexibility (75). Contracting out has the potential to lower the burden of government costs without diminishing service provision, proponents say.

The economic rationale postulating greater efficiency that is given for contracting out is rooted in the context of privatization ideology. Privatization has been at the forefront of the economic policy debate over the past fifteen years (Nkya 1995; Bailey and Rothenberg 1995; Butler 1987). Contracting out has been part of a broad appeal of privatization that promises smaller government and more reliance on private initiative (Pack 1991). According to various authors (Green 1995; Donahue 1989; Lieberman 1994; Herbst 1990), privatization has been heralded as a key aspect of current economic reforms.

An impetus for contracting out was the realization that public resources were not unlimited. Public agencies USAID included were under pressure to become more efficient. If they could not deliver the goods, then others could. Hence, the rationale for privatization is that private contractors and competitive tendering would inspire more efficient procedures, cut cost, and improve quality of service delivery (Butler 1991; Osborn and Gaebler 1992).

Proponents of contracting out contend that the government is trying to do too much and, therefore, advocate turning over government functions to private sector organizations (Bennett and Johnson 1981; McAfee and McMillan 1988; Savas 1987). The relative merit of contracting out, as seen by its proponents, is that it is a cost-efficient strategy.

Efficiency refers to the appropriate allocation of resources, that is, obtaining the greatest output per unit of input. Several authors have found evidence that for certain services private provision is cheaper (Savas 1987; Bocherding 1979; DeHoog 1984; Greene1994; Bennett and Johnson 1981; Ferris and Graddy 1986). The potential costs savings derive from economies of scale, the labor practices of private contractors, and competition among suppliers aimed at minimizing cost. However, Millward (1982) found cases for which the market provision was not always supported by the evidence. Tang (1997) also notes that there is no conclusive evidence that the private sector is more efficient than the public sector. In some areas, research findings suggest that the public sector may be more efficient than the private sector, but in others (electricity, railways) it is the other way around. In many other cases, the outcome is mixed.

The push for privatization has been based not just on economic grounds, but on political ones. The Reagan Revolution and its counterparts in other developed countries took as an a priori assumption that big government is bad government (Carroll et al. 1985). Political conservatives argued against federal programs and government intervention because they viewed the public sector as intrusive, and inefficient (Ascher 1989; Donahue 1989; Savas 1987). They also argued that government activism threatens individual rights. These conservatives also tended to be strongly pro-business, so an economic/political philosophy that stressed private business over public agencies funding social services fit neatly with their ideological bent and political constituency.

However, some observers such as Butler (1987) and Starr (1987) have expressed reservations about contracting out as a common form of privatization because they say the process simply shifts the locus of service production from the public sector to the private sector without necessarily reducing government spending. As Starr (1987) puts it, this will only create an enlarged class of private contractors and other providers dependent on public money (128). Boston (1995) also argues that as government agencies are shedding many of their delivery functions to private contractors, a growing number of public servants are spending their time managing contracts rather than delivering the services (78). Proponents would respond that if private concerns do the job better and at a lower cost, it's worth spending public money.

The move away from state-oriented development to promoting private business, which has been widespread, is often seen as a much-needed corrective to the excesses of the public sector. However, relying on the private marketplace for the delivery of public services has raised issues of values, quality, and accountability. Many economists have reservations about contracting out, because although it may offer substantial savings, it also presents numerous traps for the unwary. The use of the market provision does not always guarantee competition and reduced costs, notes King (1994). He also stresses that although in theory it may be possible to avoid losers, in reality competitive tendering and contracting out will often leave some parties worse off (75). Some of these issues include reductions in employment, worsening conditions of employment and wages, and loss of long-term expertise in the government agency, among others.

As mentioned before, an important element in the contracting process are transaction costs, which include not only the costs of writing specifications, organizing and assessing the bids, but also the costs of the design and negotiation of contracts as well as of monitoring projects (Baye and Beil 1994; Domberger and Jensen 1997; Ferris and Graddy 1991; Williamson 1979). All these administrative elements of transaction, also known as transaction cost, might be large enough to offset the benefits of private provision.

Prager (1992, 1994) argues that since contractors are rewarded for completing specific tasks, they are less likely to make decisions based on a long-term framework. Their incentives to keep costs low and profits high could mean cost cutting that compromises the quality of the project but satisfies the conditions of the contract. Moreover, he suggests that inadequate attention is being paid to the costs of managing contracts and monitoring contractor compliance by the public sector. According to Domberger and Rimmer (1994), these costs can sometimes offset or even exceed the savings generated from competitive tendering (443).

There is a growing body of literature suggesting that the impact of contracting out in the short run leads to cost reduction under different scenarios, but the impact in the long run is not entirely clear (Domberger and Rimmer 1994). For instance, firms enter bidding under competitive situations, but once a strong presence or monopoly is attained, they increase their prices. Another scenario is as follows: because of insufficient information, bidders could place excessively low bids generating an initial government cost saving, or they could purposely bid low (low balling) to win a contract, with the expectation that they will be able to recoup losses later. When contracts are renewed, bidders will increase their prices to levels that could dissipate cost savings (Hanrahan 1983; Rimmer 1994).

To the extent that contracting out is supposed to reduce expenditures on service provisions, notes Borland (1994), what is likely to be the effect of these services? Critics of contracting out claim that any observed cost savings merely reflect a decline in quality. The evidence for this, however, is not conclusive, says King (1994). Rimmer (1994) also notes that much of the existing evidence is ambiguous or contradictory. If the contracting process is led by financial considerations, then it is likely that contracts will be awarded mainly on the basis of price. Since the use of contracting out has been directly associated with the fiscal pressures facing governments, contracting out may lead to an undesirable erosion of quality (Borland 1994). However, governments do not have quality specifications prior to using contracting out, and therefore little accurate data are available about the impact of contracting out on service quality.

But even if contracting out were to lead to a lower quality in services, it may be socially desirable if this is accompanied by a fall in price. In any case, quality is multidimensional and usually difficult or impossible to measure. Often, quality must be judged by second-best measures.

When examining contracting out, it is also necessary to consider the incentives for politicians and whether they have the correct inducements to promote welfare-enhancing contracts. Domberger (1994) notes that some contractors may engage in illegal bid rigging, where suppliers collude on the prices they offer the government authority. But collusion is not only a problem of government tenders; it may also be exacerbated by problems in the tendering process itself. If collusion exists, it may reduce or eliminate any gain to the government from the contracting process.

As Rimmer and Borland both note, even when explicit collusion is absent, any gains from contracting out will be muted if the market for the provision of the relevant service is itself characterized by lack of competition (King 1994, 76-77).

If contracting out leads to cost savings to the government, Quiggin (1994) argues, they come from two sources. First, contracting out often leads to implicit or explicit reductions in wages: people are paid less or they are put in situations in which they work at greater intensity and thus achieve higher productivity results. Second, contracting out may reflect a movement of funds from one part of government to another, and thus the source of cost reduction is simply a transfer. This type of paper savings is irrelevant in the true picture of whether contracting costs less, Quiggin argues.

Arguments against contracting out point out that private contractors are often more readily able to evade taxes than public sector employees because they work non-standard hours. Since tax evasion is likely to increase by contracting out, its true social benefit is negative (DeHoog 1984; Quiggin 1994). Quiggin (1994) points out that increased work intensity intended to save money may lead to a reduction in safety procedures. In the end, a reduction in real wages may push them below their socially optimal level, resulting in a deadweight loss to society. Finally, critics have also asserted that another purpose of contracting out is to weaken the unions (Hanrahan 1987).

What can be drawn from the arguments on contracting out? Although analysts both for and against contracting out have many different viewpoints and arguments, most note that the privatization issue has to be approached cautiously and selectively. Rushing into contracting out at any level of government may lead to higher costs. According to King (1994), the decision to introduce compet-itive tendering for a government service is not a win-win situation but must be considered on a case-by-case basis. Although significant savings may be reaped (at least by the government) by sensible application of contracting out, it does not offer a panacea to public sector fiscal constraints (27).

Analysis of contracting out shows that there are advantages and disadvantages associated with it. Hanrahan (1983) and MacManus (1992) stress that some of the advantages could be reduced costs, greater flexibility and efficiency, special expertise, and no need to buy plants and equipment. At the same time, the disadvantages are reduced accountability and control, lack of real competition for contracts, and dependency on contractors (Prager 1992, 1994).

NOTE

1. As mentioned at the beginning of the text, in other countries "pri-vatization" has been mainly a matter of selling parts of an abundant stock of 'public assets'" (Donahue 1989, 6), but in the United States, privatization has had a different meaning. It mainly means enlisting the private sector, to improve the performance of the public sector, delegating *public* duties to *private* organizations.

3

The Business of Government Contracting

The ability of business groups and private contractors to influence aid policy has become increasingly noticeable. This influence stems from their expertise and the fact that they have the economic and political clout to gain the ears of policy makers. These groups have vested interests in foreign aid because it is a major business for them. The aid industry is made up of corporate executives of consulting firms, non-governmental organizations (NGOs) that depend on USAID for much of their funding, and exporting firms involved in aid-financed commodity procurement. Inside the foreign aid bureaucracy in Washington, many USAID program officials and eventually some contracting officers end up working for private contractors and consulting firms. Many of these firms also have close associations with officials who shape foreign aid policy. As is often the case in Washington, D.C., the close relationships among lobbyists and policy makers facilitate the lobbyists' interests. These businesses have built organizations designed to influence and collaborate with foreign policy officials on matters of foreign aid (Choate 1990).

This chapter begins with an overview of the mechanisms of government contracting, then describes contracting at USAID and how a relatively small group of contractors has come to dominate the process.

DOING BUSINESS WITH THE GOVERNMENT

Government contracting is big business. The U.S. government spends approximately $200 billion annually in procurement of goods and services, and this accounts for approximately one-fifth of the federal budget. This makes the U.S. government by far the largest consumer and customer for prime contract awards, including those for defense, space exploration, foreign aid, and others. The sheer size of the federal market is too important to ignore, because few markets surpass the dimensions of the U.S. government.

Private contractors represent a large and growing business. In terms of numbers, the greatest concentration of contractors is in the Washington, D.C., area. Many of these rely for nearly all their business, in terms of income, on selling to the government. Most of the large for-profit contractors are well-established firms with a staff of proposal writers, accountants, auditors, engineers, economists, and lawyers. Some of these firms can afford to spend hundreds of thousands of dollars in putting together a proposal, depending on the size of the contract. Smaller firms do not have the resources, and it is typically the chief executive officer who writes the proposal. In fact, with a definitive shift away from affirmative action and support for small disadvantaged businesses, larger, more established firms have a distinct edge.

Doing business with the government is both complex and risky. As contracting has grown rapidly over the last twenty years, it has been accompanied by increasing regulations, just as almost all parts of government have. The government guidelines that define the federal procurement process are established in the Federal Acquisition Regulation (FAR), a document of more than eight hundred pages and thousands more pages containing supplementary rules for every government agency, all of which have their own missions and statutory regulations. The extensiveness of the government's regulations prevents much discretion in awarding contracts. However, in spite of the complex regulations, doing business with the U.S. government can be a rewarding experience. Hence, understanding the federal government's market, although tricky, is crucial to doing business.

Greater regulation was also prompted by media revelations of alleged excesses in contracting (e.g., overcharging the government). Concern over inflating cost estimates and obtaining excessive profits has led to more regulations that often have been criticized as restrictive. The General Accounting Office (GAO) has noted that today, there are no statutory standards to directly regulate government contractor profits, except on an individual contract basis. The determination of profit policy, therefore, is left primarily to the agencies to address administratively (GAO 1989, 14). The GAO has recommended an appropriate analytical methodology to evaluate profitability on contracts negotiated with the federal government. Other studies have also been proposed to find out whether profitability on government contracts is compatible with commercial contractors for similar goods and services.

New procurement regulations are intended to remedy alleged contractor abuses even if at the same time they have made procurement more restrictive. Criticism has also been leveled at the federal agencies for being both negligent and inept in discovering these problems and not taking appropriate actions (GAO 1989, 1995a; U.S. Congress 1992). But contractors have usually reassessed their management strategies and adjusted to the new regulations (Alston et al. 1992).

Although a large number of contracts must be won through the formal submission of proposals and are competitive, a significant number of contracts are awarded with no or limited competition. This means that the government does not always rely on a standardized procedure with specific criteria to obtain prices that are fair and reasonable. Under these conditions, the government analyzes the validity of the contractor's proposed costs and reaches an agreement on the rate of profit. This is based on cost and price analysis, audit, and weighted guidelines (a technique to compute overall profit). The lessons used in determining the overall profitability are: profit for performance risk, profit depending on the contract type, and profit in relation to overall investment.

Although government procurement is supposed to reflect free and open competition, one of the major criticisms of its practice is that it is insufficiently competitive (GAO 1989; U.S. Congress 1992). Competition for contracts is supposed to drive down bids, and therefore, lower the cost to the government. Weak competition will tend to make cost-plus or cost-reimbursement contracts the preferred contracts. Unmotivated exclusion of firms from the right to bid for government business, or favoritism in the selection of contractors undermines competition. Procurement on sole source basis does not result in the savings one would encounter when it is done on a competitive basis. The extent of competition depends on the number of firms submitting bids and the dispersion of the firms' expected costs. The higher the number of bids and the closer their expected costs, the greater the competition.

According to a GAO report, there is a long history of concern about profits earned on government contracts. Contract prices should allow contractors to recover their costs and provide a reasonable profit to compensate for investment, risk, and effort (GAO 1989, 8).

For years, Congress has reported on contractors' unreasonable profits. Although the free market establishes what is known as a fair price to the buyer and an equitable profit to the seller, aberrations in the marketplace, such as the inability to obtain competition for certain items or services, sometimes lead to excessive profits (U.S. Congress 1992).

Facing critical issues of downsizing certain government operations (e.g., defense), private for-profit contractors have been implementing business strategies to maintain profitability. Through dubious accounting practices, they have been able to maximize their profits by mitigating adverse effects of the market and by adjusting their prices. Price adjustment is done by inflating allowable costs (planning costs, labor costs, precontract costs, service costs, material costs, travel costs, operational costs, etc.) and those that require special consideration.

Because of the large volume of business the government conducts with for-profit contracting firms, contract abuse, which has been often reported in the media, is common. One type of abuse lies in the contracts awarded without competition. This is sometimes known as selected-source or sole-source procurement. The basis of all procurement regulations is competition, but when the government selects a contractor without competition, the agency must justify the procedure. Agencies such as USAID permit selected-source procurement whenever they see it as necessary.

The most evident form of abuse in the procurement system comes from excessive cost overruns and performance inadequacies by contractors. The tales of abuse of some government contracts have been widely reported in the press (for example, the Department of Defense being charged $435 for a hammer or $659 for an ashtray). These stories have fed a pervasive cynicism about government performance and careless procurement. Over the years there has been growing criticism of government contracts that carry excessive cost overruns. The other type of abuse is the ineffectiveness of the contractors when they achieve poor results.

The growth of contracting has been fueled by the move toward a less restrictive free-market-based economy. By opening up public services to market competition, advocates of contracting stress that there is potential for saving money and improving service quality. However, contracting sometimes departs from the competitive free-market model if there is no rigorous bidding. Instead, government agencies and private for-profit contractors develop over time long-term relationships governed by their own specific norms and expectations. These relationships could influence the delivery of services and the way contracting is managed.

As the contracting relationship develops, the largest and most influential contractors develop a strong bond with government agencies. Consequently, government officials (e.g., contracting officers) may be reluctant to disturb the contracting relationship. The largest contractors have also become influential constituents, leaving the purchasing agency with little choice but to continue the contract. Although a good relationship is desirable and the government agency has developed trust in the contractor from years of dealing with the firm, terminating contracts is difficult to enforce.

According to Guttman and Willner (1976), the contracting process "is dominated by the network of relationships that exists between contractor and agency, and these relationships are crucial to many decisions in the awarding and administration of contracts" (24). Although contractors may claim to be working in "the public interest," they are foremost a business. The process of contracting often involves personal contacts between firm CEOs and people in government. For a contractor, the cultivation of inside contacts in the government is important because they provide an advantage in accessing information that others might not have. Sometimes when the government agency lacks reliable information on the consulting firm or individuals, "judgement about the capabilities of contenders is often based on firm 'name,' or personal contact" (Guttman and Willner 1976, 35).

Contractors often gain access to information that helps them win contracts. With time they gain expertise that makes them valuable and puts them in a favorable position to win more future contracts. Although contractors are perceived as outsiders, they have actually become an indispensable part of the system of support for aid programs from which they benefit.

Since contracts do not manage themselves, effective contracts require careful administration. Without adequate public administration, abuses and inefficiency are likely to surface. The rules established in the FAR provide for fair competition, which reduces the chances of corruption in the procurement process. Nowhere, however, do the regulations emphasize *excellence* in performing the job by contractors (Kelman 1994). In fact, until recently, contractors have not been concerned with performance since what is most often required of them is the *level of effort*. That is, the government asks for no more than it requires to meet its needs. However, in recent years the government has been trying to move away from these types of contracts, drawing up more contracts that require "deliverables" that are accepted or rejected. Furthermore, government agencies are under pressure to award contracts at the discretion of contracting officers but still have little concern for the monitoring and evaluation of such contracts. As Kelman (1994) makes clear, current procurement practices and regulations are thus a major source of the mediocre performance of the government suppliers (107).

Reports by the GAO, the Office of Management and Budget (OMB), and congressional hearings over the last decade indicate that there are at least three major problems with the procurement system. These are: (1) contract oversight and mismanagement, (2) auditing, and (3) cost reimbursement rules. These reports document the many serious deficiencies with government contract administration and auditing practices (U.S. Congress 1992). The reports have found instances in which contracts are being closed without audits. The findings also stress that insufficient attention is paid to seeing that the contract terms are met and that procurement regulations are followed after award. Moreover, in many other instances it was found that inflated rates were being charged in the leasing of equipment, overcharging for personnel expenses, and other questionable costs leading to cost overruns.

Deficiencies in contract administration and oversight result from several factors, including inadequate management attention (Holtz 1979). One of the problems is that the focus is on getting the job done rather than monitoring and evaluating the contracts awarded. Inadequate cost controls do lead to inflated costs. Unallowable and questionable costs presented by contractors in their proposals have been an issue of concern for some time that has not yet been properly addressed. Corrective actions and recommendations have been to strengthen contract audit management. But complicating matters has been the lack of resources that forced agencies to reduce the number of procurement personnel. Audits to ensure that the government does not pay more than a reasonable allowable amount for contracting services have not kept pace with the number of contracts awarded. The cost implications of insufficient audits lead to improper charges that have significant financial consequences to the government.

Another important issue in government contracting is the increasing concentration of the largest, more experienced contractors. These contractors, which have good inside knowledge of the trade, have been chipping away market share from their smaller counterparts. Recent figures on government contractors show that despite talk of leveling the playing field in federal procurement policy, the ten largest contractors capture approximately one-third of all government contracts. In 1996, the value of federal contracts awarded to firms in the Washington, D.C., area increased by 11.3 percent from the previous year (Deady 1997). Moreover, congressional repeals of programs that benefited small minority-and women-owned businesses have hurt small contractors.

One of the problems associated with contracts is that once a contract is won, firms negotiate contract changes to cover cost overruns and scheduling delays. After the contract has been completed contractors can even negotiate performance evaluation. The government's readiness to renegotiate contracts also adds to the problem.

CONTRACTING FOR USAID

The analysis here is primarily concerned with contractors that do development work that is solicited by USAID. These contractors are responsible through direct delegation or by joint participation with USAID for the billions of dollars allocated to development assistance. Contractors are usually selected when they have a sound proposal, and have suitable technical and managerial resources available to do the work. Now, as will be explained in chapter 6, past performance also plays a small role in the selection process.

One issue that will be discussed in greater detail later is performance-based contracting (PBC) as a method of contracting. PBC is an approach now used that seeks to utilize private sector management practices in preparing the solicitation and administering the contract. PBC is a form of managing for results that in the end means desirable contractor performance (Taber 1996). PBC is also a way of enforcing compliance because it ensures the achievement of performance targets.

USAID contracting differs in many respects from more conventional competitive bidding, and in some ways from other government agencies. One major difference is the use of cost-reimbursement contracts, predominantly cost-plus fixed fee (CPFF) level-of-effort contracts, which still account for about 80 percent of procurement outlays at the agency. Prices are generally agreed by negotiation on an estimate of actual costs, rather than being set in a competitive basis. Under CPFF, the contractor and the agency agree upon a fee or profit amount based upon an estimate of total costs. The agency agrees to reimburse within limits all allowable costs incurred by the contractor.

The enduring problems in the management of the agency have been exposed in GAO reports and congressional hearings. Press accounts have also criticized the agency. By 1996, it was on the brink of extinction, and barely escaped being dissolved by Congress. Albeit slowly, the agency has been under reform since 1994, when Brian Atwood assumed the administration of the agency. However, problems still plague USAID because it is being asked to do more with less. Despite the considerable effort expended to streamline the procurement process, the changes are not easy and do not come quickly. Under budget pressures and the challenge to produce measurable results, the agency has failed to provide the necessary staff training to keep abreast of the new regulations as established in the revised Federal Acquisition Regulation (FAR). These problems are also common to all federal agencies.

Another issue that becomes apparent in the procurement process at USAID is the long-term relationships with certain well-established vendors, which discourages the agency from shopping around for the lowest price. Sometimes contracting officers are not trusted to use their own good judgment because the system limits them or because they are now too complacent to pursue incentive type contracts that might be more appropriate under certain circumstances. Contracting officers are often reluctant to deal with newcomers who might need some guidance. The evidence shows that the government varies very little in its purchasing patterns from year to year, even if there is a degree of complexity in procurement.

The agency favors using technical assistance experts to work on development projects who are known to them from past dealings. This reflects a certain mistrust of local qualified expertise and brainpower. The mistrust is often shared by local governments who have more faith in foreign contractors than their own local experts. Another reason why there is a preference for American contractors is because of their size and their ability to respond immediately to a particular need, irrespective of the cost. Finally, there are legal restrictions on contracts for the acquisition of goods and services. FAR part 25 defines the Buy American Act, which restricts USAID in procuring goods from foreign sources.

More often than not, less developed countries (LDCs) accept technical assistance as it is supplied to them. Most countries do not negotiate their assistance. It's provided by the donor through its country mission as officials see fit. The contracts are normally awarded to contractors or consultancy firms from the donor country. Development contractors usually recruit their personnel for a project or program from a list of experts on their files, but they do their hiring only when a contract has been awarded. Temporary appointments are a way of reducing the firm's overhead.

According to a GAO (1994) report, one significant area of weakness has been USAID's oversight of contractor performance. Although the agency has gradually established an in-country presence through its missions to implement projects or programs, its procurement system is still plagued with logistical delays, high administrative costs, and consumer dissatisfaction. Since USAID relies on outside private contractors to manage its assistance activities, the agency staff is more preoccupied with contract management and loses touch with the reality of field work. Another problem that emerges is the supervision of contractors because sometimes different firms handle separate phases of the same project. As one of the National Performance Review (NPR) reports (1993b) puts it, a project could be designed by one contractor, implemented by another, and redesigned by still another contractor (37).

USAID pays contractors at U.S. rates for work that LDC local organizations might be able to do at the local rate for a fraction of the cost. Although U.S. contractors are needed in countries where technical expertise is lacking, there is a definite advantage in using the growing reservoir of host country professionals to assist with development projects. Incentives to encourage U.S. contractors to form partnerships with local organizations as a way of strengthening institutional capabilities have not been fully pursued (Sogge and Zadek 1996).

Canada's IDRC (International Development Research Centre) has as its main mission the belief that the problems of LDCs cannot be solved by importing outside solutions. The IDRC promotes development by providing funds to developing country researchers who are working within their own country on solutions to their nations' problems. This approach offers research opportunities that build up scientific capacity. A similar approach is used by the Swedish Agency for Research and Economic Cooperation with Developing Countries (SAREC).

These views have also been expressed eloquently by Berg (1997), who stresses that aid in its present form often undermines local institutional development and capacity building. These negative effects persist, as he puts it, not because donors lack awareness of them. Although donors often talk in terms of working in partnership, there is inconsistency in the rhetoric when they insist on their own agendas (e.g., conditionality and tighter and more formal rules on how aid is to be allocated).

MARKET CONCENTRATION AND CONTRACTOR BEHAVIOR

Market Structure of USAID Contractors

The market structure of contractors competing for USAID contracts has oligopolistic characteristics. An important feature of this market is the small number of firms that are awarded the bulk of contracts, both in number and in dollar value. The strategic behavior of these firms leaves little room for the smaller less established contractors to win contracts. The impediments to entry for new firms are their lack of resources (small staff, less cash flow, unwillingness to take risks) and the technical sophistication of the larger more established firms. Scale economies make it unprofitable for more than a few firms to dominate the market for the larger, and most profitable contracts.

Table 3.1 lists the top twenty five firms that were awarded most of the contracts from 1991 to 1995. The data show the number of contracts obtained by these firms per year and the dollar value of these contracts. The concentration of these is evident in the percentage of all contracts accounted for by the largest and most active firms in this market. The nature of the market structure provides useful insight as to the competitiveness and procurement practices in the development aid business.

The large number of contracts awarded to these twenty five firms suggests that they have market power, since the smaller the number of contractors, the larger, on average, is the share of the market supplied by individual vendors. Since the market is segmented, the number of firms is likely to influence behavior, because members of the small group involved know each other, are familiar with one another's operations, and can predict with some accuracy the behavior of rivals.

Another aspect of concentration is evident in Table 3.2, which provides a regional breakdown of the fifty states plus the District of Columbia, Puerto Rico, and the Virgin Islands. The region with the greatest geographical concentration of contractors is the District of Columbia, Maryland, and Virginia. The data reveal that in both dollar value and number of contracts, the Washington, D.C. area is where most contracting firms are based. These two states and the District of Columbia account for more than half of all contracts awarded by USAID. The dependence on their income coming from USAID is such that some of the firms rely exclusively or for most of their income on the agency. In fact, some of these firms are situated in the same building as USAID, across the street, or around the corner from it.[1] All these firms are mostly for-profit contractors. The non-profit organizations receive mainly grants, although an increasing number of them are also competing for contracts (Robinson 1997). There is a broad diversity among NGOs, and the

Table 3.1
USAID's 25 Largest Contractors

Contractors	FY 1991		FY 1992		FY 1993	
	No. of Contracts	Contract Value	No. of Contracts	Contract Value	No. of Contracts	Contract Value
Abt Associates	22	28,047,123.00	52	37,434,409.00	17	20,213,559.84
Academy for Educational Development	39	182,774,998.00	63	295,367,515	28	148,472,981.41
Agricultural Cooperative Development Intl.	11	24,462,259.00	20	44,447,837.00	5	11,084,705
Aguirre International	4	29,152,780.00	7	32,284,951.15	5	7,794,227.80
Arthur Andersen			3	136,484.56		
Associates in Rural Development	11	19,674	20	20,954,256.00	20	3,276,788.19
Booz-Allen and Hamilton					3	30,092,252.00
Chemonics International, Inc.	19	49,966,974.00	44	87,463,853.64	45	58,428,986.27
Coopers and Lybrand Associates	13	22,054,672.00	35	31,323,144.86	14	32,391,755.00
Deloitte and Touche	9	18,938,649.55	29	36,230,329.78	32	75,740,420.00
Development Alternatives, Inc.	29	60,154,400.00	77	110,620,397.00	33	38,044,451.69
Development Associates, Inc.	10	36,217,887.00	29	73,382,311.93	23	12,015,007.18
DevTech, Inc.	4	3,120,823.00	3	2,202,514.00	4	7,866,692.00
Futures Group, Inc.	25	63,122,036.73	59	88,026,588.00	22	15,130,494.00
International Resources Group, ltd.	18	36,852,850.00	18	18,483,251.00		
Intl. Science & Technology Inst., Inc	17	32,494,726.00	30	48,236,588.00	21	9,222,218.00
John Snow, Inc.	20	105,436,454.00	40	89,204,242.74	30	65,134,381.79
KPMG Peat Marwick	3	9,031,018.00	37	24,886,627.20	51	69,170,983.21
Louis Berger International, Inc.	11	42,669,561.00	16	68,430,620.00	3	1,582,822.00
Macro International, Inc.			13	34,216,504.00	8	4,743,971.61
Management Systems International	19	5,842,950.00	53	16,956,772.00	47	13,686,092.40
Nathan Associates, Inc.	12	12,013,749.00	10	6,638,112.14	13	8,788,232.00
PADCO	7	8,321,630	14	19,275,538.00	9	695,801.00
Price Waterhouse	27	26,162,314.23	134	69,337,605.59	92	54,759,639.85
RCG/Hagler Bailly, Inc.	3	3,773,604.00	8	20,913,879.00	9	82,919,948.07
TOTAL	333	800,631,132.51	814	1,276,454,331.59	534	771,256,410.31

Contractors	FY 1994 No. of Contracts	FY 1994 Contract Value	FY 1995 No. of Contracts	FY 1995 Contract Value	FY 1996 No. of Contracts	FY 1996 Contract Value
Abt Associates	29	124,632,225.00	40	139,499,974.00	28	129,094,461.00
Academy for Educational Development	57	546,946,665.56	51	549,577,597.00	69	275,325,613.00
Agricultural Cooperative Development Intl.	22	57,190,988.17	19	51,637,586.00	23	53,306,660.00
Aguirre International	18	15,702,387.91	22	17,875,608.00	17	16,372.53
Arthur Andersen	2	46,055,180.00	7	52,834,879.00	7	46,383,043.00
Associates in Rural Development	25	34,625,588.00	26	53,021,661.00	28	66,026,426.00
Booz-Allen and Hamilton	5	33,669,040.00	10	47,832,650.00	20	59,224,992.00
Chemonics International, Inc.	58	155,489,625.00	72	240,039,325.00	149	272,246,041.00
Coopers and Lybrand Associates	37	30,675,593.00	47	38,401,327.00	62	36,127,586.00
Deloitte and Touche	49	98,512,976.59	30	97,327,096.06	16	107,080,547.00
Development Alternatives, Inc.	58	88,051,289.00	53	144,407,912	65	134,533,415
Development Associates, Inc.	31	73,495,619.00	31	81,141,548.21	43	62,843,523.00
DevTech, Inc.	7	8,920,906.00	13	12,078,756.29	19	16,066,371.00
Futures Group, Inc.	51	97,654,817.64	58	123,567,783.00	38	104,521,115.00
International Resources Group, ltd.	11	55,832,205.90	6	56,870,555.40	9	61,770,283.00
Int. Science & Technology Inst., Inc	22	45,775,262.25	17	25,793,609.00	18	779,024.00
John Snow, Inc.	43	137,560,328.71	31	206,258,928.31	30	23,546,438.00
KPMG Peat Marwick	56	180,105,617.00	71	216,822,340.00	26*	214,701,993.00
Louis Berger International, Inc.	16	39,822,494.00	11	30,969,122.00	21	28,840,072.00
Macro International, Inc.	12	60,739,292.00	12	41,925,985.00	16	49,365,433.00
Management Systems International	81	31,742,271.69	71	26,953,454.08	76	38,211,057.00
Nathan Associates, Inc.	15	26,392,166.00	20	66,170,128.00	11**	34,345,151.00
PADCO	19	41,924,602.00	13	34,205,488.00	23	66,521,050.00
Price Waterhouse	106	125,169,769.00	71	95,098,692.12	82	105,765,900.00
RCG/Hagler Bailly, Inc.	24	68,096,200.00	27	99,847,178.00	26	92,121,429.00
TOTAL	854	2,224,822,909.42	829	2,550,159,182.24	885	2,078,763,995.53

* KPMG/Berents Groups; ** also Nathan Associates/Burlington North.

Source: USAID, Division of Procurement, Yellow Books 1991, 1992, 1993, 1994, 1995, 1996

Table 3.2
Geographical Concentration of Contractors *

	FY 1991			FY 1992			FY 1993		
	# contracts	%	$ value	# contracts	%	$ value	# contracts	%	$ value
Total of 48 states**	1110	54%		1776	48%		1893	48%	
District of Columbia	602	29%	$ 1,691,950,762	1139	31%	$ 2,474,798,774	1228	31%	$ 2,901,970,926
Maryland	166	8%	$ 360,513,319	323	9%	$ 436,601,056	319	8%	$ 525,019,989
Virginia	179	9%	$ 422,202,108	439	12%	$ 721,586,448	498	13%	$ 793,345,878
Total for Washington, DC area	947	46%	$ 2,474,666,189	1901	52%	$ 3,632,986,278	2045	52%	$ 4,220,336,792
Overall Total	2057	100%		3677	100%		3938	100%	

	FY 1994			FY 1995			FY 1996		
	# contracts	%	$ value	# contracts	%	$ value	# contracts	%	$ value
Total of 48 states**	1789	47%		1751	46%		1553	45%	
District of Columbia	1208	32%	$ 4,143,097,385	1202	32%	$ 4,418,811,513	1124	32%	$ 4,346,953,100
Maryland	329	9%	$ 686,438,865	337	9%	$ 797,906,852	298	9%	$ 834,229,698
Virginia	501	13%	$ 936,132,050	508	13%	$ 1,072,746,372	497	14%	$ 1,161,346,995
Total for Washington, DC area	2038	53%	$ 5,765,668,299	2049	54%	$ 6,289,464,737	1919	55%	$ 6,342,529,792
Overall Total	3827	100%		3800	100%		3472	100%	

* Refers to contracts, grants and cooperative agreements received by all for-profit and non-profit organizations.

** Includes Puerto Rico and U.S. Virgin Islands

Source: Yellow Book fiscal years 1991, 1992, 1993, 1994, 1995, 1996, USAID Office of Procurement, Contract Management System

nature of the work of many of them is mainly humanitarian and relief effort, with development playing a less important role in their overall mission.

An interesting aspect of firm concentration is the prevalence of four of accounting's big six (Coopers and Lybrand, Price Waterhouse, KPMG Peat Marwick, and Deloitte and Touche). As business consulting is outpacing auditing as the primary growth area for accounting firms, these firms have established a strong presence in the emerging markets of Eastern and Central Europe. The demise of state socialism in Eastern and Central Europe resulted in the transformation of these centrally planned economies into market-driven ones based on private ownership. As privatization, liberalization, and macroeconomic adjustment policies became important features of the transformation, these firms have been playing a bigger role in providing management consultancy in private sector strategies. In fact, USAID data show that a significant amount of aid through contracts, not only to LDCs but to Eastern Europe, now goes to improve market imperfections.

For privatization efforts in particular, USAID has used IQC (indefinite quantity contracts) types of contracts, which have been awarded mostly to the top four accounting firms. Each firm has a consortium of subcontractors, some of whom are also part of the top twenty five firms. One of the main features of IQCs used in Eastern Europe is the fixed daily rates, which are set for functional labor categories. Each rate includes the salary cost or consulting fee of the individual performing the service plus other costs such as benefits and per diem. Under these contracts, the firm bills the agency at specified daily rates (e.g., the daily rate for an attorney at KPMG Peat Marwick is $1,350). The ceiling for each firm is $30 million.

The primary reason why USAID selected IQC-types of contracts was to provide assistance quickly and to maintain flexibility. However, according to a GAO (1994) report, government officials of the host countries noted that the agency has not always met these goals. The main conclusion of the GAO report was that USAID oversight of contractor performance under IQC contracts has been inadequate. It was noted in the report that the agency has not kept complete records of project activities. On the other hand, contractors also did not maintain project files relating to decision papers, authorizations, waivers, correspondence, implementation reports, audits, and evaluations or trip records. Interestingly, GAO had made note of these issues in a 1993 report, but the pattern went unnoticed, or at least uncorrected.

Firm Behavior in Contracting for USAID

A revealing feature of contractors working with USAID is the market behavior of these firms. Instead of competing against one another, some firms are teaming up to work jointly, with erstwhile or current rivals, particularly in large multiyear contracts. Most economists support the concept of competition and encourage the federal government to expand its use in the determination of contract awards. However, as contracts are fewer but larger in value, the competing vendors are ready to cooperate or form legal partnerships and agree on ways of negotiating jointly to win and split the contract. In cases when there are only two or three firms bidding for a large contract, and they cooperate and combine, the firms might reap benefits based on their comparative advantage. This type of cooperation occurs when firms reach an explicit agreement to divide or share the market, to fix prices, or otherwise restrict competition among themselves. This collusive behavior may permit firms to reduce uncertainty, increase profits, and restrict competition. One case in point is the Basics Project, in which a five-year contract valued at $50 million was split in a legal partnership among three contractors that normally would bid separately to win the contract.

Teaming arrangements confirm a change in attitude among the largest contractors. This is a potentially cost-saving mechanism to reduce fixed costs because formulating the proposal, bidding, and negotiations are costly procedures. Partnerships are now seen as opportunities, or the price you have to pay to get the contract. Contenders for large contracts are involved in marketing, lobbying, and designing strategies to adapt to changes and win contracts.

Many of the senior contract administration staff of these contracting firms are former government officials; some of them have even worked for USAID earlier in their careers as project officers and in some cases as contracting officers.[2] They are attractive to private for-profit contractors because of their expertise and inside knowledge of how the government operates. Many of them have several years of experience in government contracting, retain the inside contacts, and are especially adept at securing contracts because they know their way in and out of the government.

NOTES

1. When the data for this book was collected in 1997-98 the Division of Procurement of USAID was in Arlington, Virgina, across from the Potomac. The agency has since moved to the Ronald Reagan Building in Washington, D.C.

2. Although there is a two-year restriction on a USAID contracting officer's going to work for a firm that is contracting for USAID, he or she can work for other contracting firms and later work for a USAID contractor.

4

Dispelling Some Foreign Aid Myths

Many factors influence the development aid process. Increasingly, USAID has become more focused on its role as a provider of domestic jobs than as a means of facilitating development in other countries. Its promise to advance private U.S. concerns and open the way for future U.S. investment now shapes USAID's promotional literature. For instance, in one of its brochures, the agency stresses that, "the principal beneficiary of American foreign assistance programs has always been the United States. Close to 80 percent of USAID's contracts and grants flow back to American firms" (USAID, n.d.). The same message is emphasized in another USAID newsletter under the title "Foreign Aid: What's in It for You?"

THE DEVELOPMENT MACHINE AND CONTRACTORS

The role of commercial interests in government aid has often been a muted issue that many in the aid industry do not want to discuss. However, when USAID had to argue its case against hostile political forces that wanted to dissolve the agency in the mid-1990s, its public relations branch proclaimed loudly on Capitol Hill that there is a legitimate place for business interests in aid, both in terms of the direct returns to the domestic economy and the role business can play in promoting development. Hoy (1998) notes that "aid is no longer evaluated in terms of the benefits to developing country recipients, but rather in terms of how it helps the United States' own self-interests" (38). InterAction, an umbrella organization representing more than 150 non-governmental organizations (NGOs) that advocates for more USAID funding launched the following argument in one of its brochures:"Myth: most foreign aid is spent in foreign countries. Reality: much of the foreign aid budget is spent in the United States. For example, roughly 90 percent of food aid is spent on U.S. goods and services. In addition, millions of foreign aid dollars go to programs that specifically promote investment and export opportunities for U.S. businesses" (InterAction, n.d.).

In recent years, commercial considerations have begun playing an increasing role in foreign development assistance policy. The emphasis in U.S. development assistance is not exclusively on sustained development. What drives this aid are mainly strategic and political concerns, as well as economic and commercial considerations (domestic jobs and the opening of market opportunities abroad). The aid industry has incentives to keep the projects going, and does not necessarily expect recipients to become self-sufficient and stop requesting aid. That would put them out of business. The aid industry employs tens of thousands of people to fulfill a broad range of economic and humanitarian objectives.

Insofar as development assistance is supposed to serve development purposes, the lines have become more blurred. In practice, development goals are secondary in importance because it is the donor's interests in satisfying its domestic constituencies that is pursued. With the demise of the Cold War, Washington has been promoting a model of free market global capitalism where foreign aid in the "new world order" is left to the private sector to function as an engine of growth rather than to government-run foreign aid programs (Grant and Nijman, 1998).

During the past fifteen years, development assistance has changed in a fundamental way. First, private for-profit contractors have come to play an important role in what is now known as the development business. Second, NGOs or non-profit organizations have proliferated and play a more active role in the development process. The relative importance of NGOs and contractors within USAID is now approximately the same. In 1992, only 9 percent of USAID's development assistance was channeled to NGOs (OECD 1995b). By 1996, 34 percent of development assistance (about 30 of ODA) were programmed through NGOs (Randel and German 1997). As Tvedt (1998) had anticipated, under the Clinton administration support to NGOs was due to increase from 13 to 50 percent of USAID's budget in 1996 (1). In the same year, USAID intro-

duced a New Partnership Initiative to involve more NGOs in its programs. The aim of this new initiative was also to strengthen linkages
between NGOs, the private sector, and the government.

Since USAID began to emphasize its role as a facilitator of development contracts to U.S. firms, more of its resources have been
going to private for-profit contractors. The agency favors contracts
as the principal means of project and program implementation, in
which even NGOs (also known as public service contractors) are
competing in greater numbers (Robinson 1997). NGOs have
increased their activities in some areas to assist the agency in exe-
cuting its own projects and programs, but as funding becomes
scarce, they are also participating more frequently in bidding for
contracts.

The emphasis on delivery of assistance in the form of contracts
has given contractors greater influence on USAID's programs and
projects. As contractors have become more involved in the provision of development aid, they have also increased their influence on
the agency's procurement operations. The more visible presence of
contractors led the agency to create a private sector promotion division in which businesses are coached on how to compete successfully for contracts (Corwin 1994). Development aid, according to
one observer, is being influenced by small but influential interest
groups who lobby "for U.S. companies that could profit from foreign
aid—either from profitable contracts or from preferential treatment
to supply goods and services" (Hecht 1996a, 1063). This trend indicates that private for-profit development contractors are becoming
the important agents influencing the course of development assistance.

Contractors (both for-profit firms and NGOs) are competing for
funding, affecting the behavior of some NGOs, which are being
forced to become more commercial in orientation. Pressured to
compete among themselves and with for-profit contractors for their
funding, many NGOs have become more "businesslike" in their
structures and operation, less autonomous and less able to under-
take certain kinds of projects (Sogge and Zadek 1996). Hence
NGOs interested in, for instance, small-scale agricultural coopera-
tives that promote self-reliance rather than market-based programs
find it more difficult to procure funding for such projects (Crook
1996). NGOs sometimes find that working as subcontractors is the

only way for them to get additional funding. As subcontractors they may find themselves compelled to pursue approaches not in accord with their philosophical and/or technical approaches to development (Hoy 1998; Overseas Development Institute 1996; Tvedt 1997). Finally, there is the charge that their efforts to satisfy the government's needs as public sector contractors could inhibit their ability to critically assess and comment on foreign aid policy for fear of "biting the hand that feeds them" (Hoy 1998, 109).

The aid industry and its largest clients in Washington, D.C. have become not only influential private organizations, but also the main beneficiaries of economic assistance programs. A former USAID official recounts that "aid distribution is just another big, private business that relies on government contracts" (Maren 1997, 8). The discourse of "corporate efficiency" and "professional consultants" is now predominant. Private for-profit contractors as well as NGOs and some PVOs see USAID as a source of funds, jobs, and influence (Saxby 1996). Projects in LDCs funded by USAID are a preferential target of development contractors because they carry attractive and profitable contracts. Kimaru (1996) claims that it is not an exaggeration to argue that a large part of aid awarded through contracts is skinned off by consultants and experts who pay themselves exorbitant fees. Others who benefit from the aid business are CEOs of NGOs and subcontractors who charge hefty fees for their "expertise." The cost for development services are high. In the end, the largest fraction of every dollar ends up as income of contractors and subcontractors, and never reaches those most in need. Both Maren (1997) and Hancock (1989) provide many examples of this. Hancock (1989) states that "today 70 cents of every dollar of American 'assistance to the Third World' never actually leave the United States" (156). He claims that USAID spends billions of dollars a year "purchasing goods and services from domestic companies and contractors," and that USAID loudly boasts that thousands of jobs are created "here at home."

The increasing reliance on outsiders (for-profit contractors and NGOs) has become well established during the past fifteen years. But relying on development experts and consultants has a high price tag, because their fees for overhead cost are "excessively inflated" (Hancock 1989). The valuable donor dollars that go to experts and consultants represent perhaps the biggest slice of official development aid budgets. Why are experts and consultants paid hefty salaries despite the large pool of such people ready to do this type of work? USAID and other aid agencies keep the fees high instead of relying on supply and demand to regulate the fees for such services. Not only are these vast sums spent on the consulting fees of contractors, but the contracting packages come with all sorts of perks for travel expenses, lodging, and local transport. For instance, per diem for a consultant subcontracted by the firm awarded the contract to go to Mozambique would be more than $300, whereas the annual per capita income in Mozambique is less than $100. Air travel could include a stopover in Paris, and, once in Maputo, the access to a Land Cruiser. Although many of these jobs could be done by locals at lower prices, the agency is sometimes unimaginative; or perhaps in its eagerness to provide business to American firms and its subcontractors, it puts less emphasis on the real cost. Furthermore, it plays down the inefficiency of U.S. firms that lack the commitment and experience that local LDCs organizations might have (Maren 1997). As Wedel (1998b), puts it, "many of these firms appeared to be more concerned with representing the interests of their clients back home than those of the countries they allegedly came to help" (63).

In post-communist Poland, these type of fly-in, fly-out contractors were known as "The Marriott Brigade" because they normally stayed at the Marriott Hotel, the most expensive in Warsaw, in town just for a few days to talk to key government officials (Wedel 1998b). One of the main tasks USAID undertook through its hired consultants was to help in the privatization effort and economic restructuring. Later, the agency expanded its priorities to include the setting up of stock exchanges, and writing up tax and environmental legislation. The agency, along with other multilateral organizations, was committed to transforming entire economies according to an image of Western capitalism. A government report noted that the U.S. obligated three quarters of its aid to privatization, private sector-development, and economic restructuring, more than any other single effort (U.S. Department of State 1996). One result of the privatization effort was that insiders acquired enterprises or parts thereof as their own private property at basement prices. Privatization opened up opportunities for abuse and corruption in the free-for-all scramble to the market (Wedel 1998a,b).

Contractors who are awarded contracts to carry out a specific project put together a team that is recruited only for the duration of a specific job. The members of the team typically have not worked together before and are there just to provide specific skills or work experience. Hancock (1989) argues that most of these consultants are not committed to the country in question and therefore have no particular interest in transferring their "indispensable" knowledge or skills to the locals. There is an uncoordinated relationship in much of the aid delivery because of the fly-in, fly-out nature in the work of USAID's paid consultants. Hence, project aid that relies on the "expertise" and advice of contractors and their hired subcontractors often makes little contribution to the development process. Hancock notes that some audited projects that have had the explicit objective of assisting the rural poor were found "to have been devised without any understanding of the problems that poor people actually face. As a result, most of these projects were abject failures" (147). In the case of Central and Eastern Europe, Wedel (1998b) says that "consultants often came with little knowledge of the countries in which they were to intervene or the contexts of the problems they were to address" (56). Indeed, many of the private for-profit contractors who went to Central and Eastern Europe came with ready solutions that did not take into account the planned nature of these economies.

Although NGOS are technically and legally nonprofit, many of these organizations doing development work are increasingly competing and collaborating with for-profit contractors to obtain lucrative contracts. They often behave like for-profit organizations. The competition has become somewhat complicated by the fact that private for-profit firms are now doing what had been the domain of NGOs, while some NGOs, under increasing financial pressure, are expanding into the competitive contracting activities of private for-profit firms. For NGOs, there are financial benefits to be gained from such relationships with private firms because they provide a way to obtain additional resources.

During the last two decades, the number of northern NGOs has grown exponentially. Tvedt (1998) estimates that there are "about 4000 development NGOs in OECD member countries." Based on USAID data, there were 434 NGOs/PVOs in the United States registered with the agency in 1996. Many of these organizations do not rely on USAID for funding and opt to seek money from other sources. But as government grants and donations from private sources decrease because of stiffer competition, the lure of commercial revenue becomes more attractive for many NGOs. In a survey of these organizations conducted by the agency, in which there were 130 respondents, 108 or 82 percent said that they had received at one point or another funding support from USAID. However, USAID funding to NGOs/PVOs continues to be highly concentrated in a relatively small number of organizations. USAID data on the total estimated cost awarded to NGOs and the portion awarded to the top twenty, top ten, and top five recipients are listed on Table 4.1. This information shows that a small group of recipients, or the top twenty organizations received 85 percent of the total money awarded in 1992 and 70 percent in 1996; the top ten received 66 percent of the total disbursed in 1992 and 51 percent in 1996.

Although the goals of nonprofits may well differ from those of private for-profit contractors, both rely heavily on the U.S. government (USAID) for the bulk of their income. Thus NGOs are confronted with a dilemma in pursuit of their development mission. On the one hand, they face increasing financial constraints and, on the other, they are engaging in contracting that might lead to a distortion of their mission (Robinson 1997; Tvedt 1998; Weisbrod 1998). Some try to maintain their integrity, but others engage in dubious fund-raising practices (e g., Save the Children, CARE) and contracting activities uncharacteristic of their non-profit image (Maren 1997). Some of these organizations run full-page ads in glossy magazines such as the *New York Times Sunday Magazine* with photographs of malnourished children, stressing that your contributions will go directly to starving or needy children when in fact much of the money they receive is spent in administrative costs and staff salaries. Maren (1997) calls this "exploitation of children for fundraising."

An important part of the debate on foreign aid centers on the effectiveness of such aid in promoting development. As the following section makes clear, there are difficulties in measuring effectiveness. In this sense, the impact of U.S. development assistance is hard to assess, because the focus now has clearly changed in favor of prescriptions for development to be directed to more free-mar-

Table 4.1
Share of USAID Funding to NGOs/PVOs by Top Recipients

	FY1992	FY1993	FY1994	FY1995	FY1996
Total to all NGOs	$786,787,518	$778,868,957	$1,086,772,209	$767,619,925	685,527,425
$ to top 20	$665,063,350	$645,967,558	$813,116,196	$626,651,509	$476,886,179
% to top 20	85%	83%	75%	82%	70%
$ to top 10	$519,850,886	$491,759,473	$637,680,398	$$461,540,625	$350,707,169
% to top 10	66%	63%	59%	60%	51%
$ to top 5	$379,023,745	$347,081,514	$479,516,721	$307,556,731	$228,884,248
% to top 5	48%	45%	44%	40%	33%

Source: USAID Advisory Committe on Voluntary Foreign Aid. *An Assessment of the State of the USAID/PVO Partnership,* June 1997, p. 37.

ket economics (and politics). As private for-profit contractors have become more frequent recipients of foreign aid dollars, USAID has been under pressure from these private interest groups, commonly known in the Washington capital as "Beltway Bandits," who attempt to exert their influence in charting the course of development assistance.

Since much of the aid is increasingly legitimized in terms of enhancing the role of business in development, it is private interest groups that have the inside track when it comes to USAID procurement. The rallying cry in Washington has been, "Business does it better." But as Eaton (1996) argues, the "experiment of 'privatizing' foreign aid has shown that the private sector does not offer a guaranteed cure for problems that critics say have plagued traditional foreign assistance programs: mismanagement, ineffectiveness, political infighting, and conflicts of interest" (A1).

EFFECTIVENESS OF DEVELOPMENT AID

How much foreign aid has actually contributed to the economic and social progress of LDCs is a question that remains largely unanswered. Some of the issues that have generated much discussion revolve around the effectiveness of the kind of aid discussed above. Effectiveness is a measure of whether goals or objectives have been met. Now aid organizations are being asked to show *performance* to continue receiving funds to provide development aid. In this sense, aid effectiveness has become the central focus of development assistance. Under increased pressure from their national legislatures, development agencies are being asked to show that foreign aid to LDCs produces results that are worth the cost. Accountability for effectiveness is predicated in the aid discourse as an efficient way to get "money for value" and as a way of convincing politicians of the merits of aid in the long run.

The effectiveness of aid is often hard to assess because different groups assign different purposes to their aid and judge its results by different criteria. Aid can be judged in terms of whether it fosters better political links, enhances the donors' commercial interest, or staves off disaster, but this is obviously not the same as judging how much it contributes to development. The arguments on the effectiveness of aid have focused mainly on how aid has, or has not, contributed to promoting development, and on how it is often misused (Berkman 1996; Boone 1995; Kraus 1983; Serageldin 1993).

Aid practitioners who work for USAID or NGOs often cite many successes in specific cases, but others have also provided evidence of mismanagement in procurement leading to practices of waste, fraud, and abuse. Specific instances have been documented in testimonies by USAID whistle-blowers or have been made public through the press. One such instance involves the allegations made by Paul Neiffer regarding USAID's contracting practices in South Africa, where there was a pattern of fraud and abuse in procurement (U.S. Government, 1996). Other instances include the gross misuse of funds that were invested in "privatization" schemes resulting in a loss of two-thirds of such an investment portfolio (Eaton 1997). In another instance, investigators uncovered misuse of money by the Harvard Institute for International Development of money intended for Russia (Myers 1997). Wedel (1998a,b) also has documented instances in which much of the money earmarked for Russia and the Newly Independent States (NIS) has been stolen or misused.

Studies on foreign aid have produced contradictory and inconclusive findings. Wood (1996), for instance, notes that "a half a century of aid programs in LDCs has not yielded any firm conclusion about the relationship between aid and development. Statistical studies have produced inconsistent and inconclusive findings" (26). One of the biggest reasons for the lack of sound information on aid effects is the gross lack of evaluation results. Riddell (1987) also argues that the available evidence does not substantiate the claims of either proponents or critics of aid because little is known about its effects. Above all, he argues, evaluation methods need to be improved. There is, however, evidence that some aid has been productive and helpful to development (Cassen and Associates 1986; Development Committee 1986; Riddell 1987). The most notable specific successes of aid programs have been in the reduction of infant mortality, the reduction of disease through immunization programs, the implementation of literacy programs, and the construction of basic infrastructure. At the same time, there are aspects of aid performance in which the results have been mixed: its contribution to spurring economic growth, to alleviating poverty, and to enhancing local technical capacity.

On economic growth, even the widely respected Cassen Report says that "inter-country statistical analyses do not show anything conclusive about the impact of aid on growth" (Cassen and Associates 1986, 33). The empirical evidence presented stresses that the contribution to economic growth and development depends on the specific country, the period of study, and the methods used for measuring and evaluating the aid programs studied, and cannot be generalized (Cassen and Associates 1986). Economists such as Krueger, Michalopoulos, and Ruttan (1989) provide a less positive view than the Cassen Report, but they also argue that the results depend on individual countries and on individual projects. Other economists such as Mosley (1987) also conclude that empirically there was no "statistically significant correlation between aid and the growth rate of GNP in developing countries" (636). Boone (1995) reached similar conclusions, claiming that aid goes into consumption and provides no impetus for growth. The policy implication of the findings of Mosley and his colleagues is that "donors should concentrate their aid in countries in which the 'effectiveness' of that aid is high" (636). Burnside and Dollar (1997) find that aid is ineffective except in a good policy environment.

The effectiveness of aid in alleviating poverty also is mixed. Although growth is important in reducing poverty, it alone is not a sufficient condition for eliminating poverty. In some countries (e.g., Korea) aid has made a contribution to poverty reduction, but a similar proportion of poverty reduction in other areas, such as Africa, has simply not occurred (Kimaru 1996). Moreover, according to the *Human Development Report* (UNDP 1996), the absolute numbers of people in poverty in LDCs are increasing.

In terms of the effectiveness of technical assistance, research shows that such aid has often failed to fully achieve its intended purpose. The question of strengthening institutional national capacity has been a subject of much controversy, and generalizations are difficult to draw. For instance, in agricultural research there have been success stories, but in other areas there have been shortcomings in the effective development of indigenous capacity. There are national policy statements from a number of countries funded by United Nations Development Program (UNDP) and based mainly in Africa, which claim that the effectiveness of technical cooperation in terms of transferring knowledge and reinforcing technical capacity has been limited.[1] The shortcomings, as stated in these national assessments, often point to the design, coordination, and implementation of projects (UNDP 1989). A number of reports note dissatisfaction with technical cooperation because aid agencies failed to pay sufficient attention to the long-term task of building local capacity. A recurrent theme is "the concern about persistent reliance on expatriate technical personnel even when suitably qualified nationals are available" (Berg 1993,5).

The misuse of aid, or its negligible impact, has drawn much criticism (Bauer and Yamey 1982; Boone 1995; White 1996). But most of the criticism focuses on recipient countries and not on how aid is disbursed. The perception of ineffectiveness often has the effect of diminishing support for development assistance. This was particularly the case when bilateral aid was used to support "friendly regimes" during the Cold War, irrespective of whether they were repressive or corrupt. Press accounts abound describing how politically motivated aid has been diverted, failing to reach the intended beneficiaries or those most in need. Similar claims are being made about aid distribution in the post-Cold War era.

The collapse of socialism in Eastern Europe resulted in promised Western aid in the billions of dollars. But in channeling the aid the donors encountered a complex system of patronage and social relations (Bruno 1998; Wedel 1998a,b). In the case of Russia, the aid was entrusted to a single group known as the "Chubais clan," which worked closely with the Harvard Institute for International Development (HIID). According to a GAO report (1996b), not only did HIID have "substantial control of the U.S. assistance program" (17), but the money awarded to HIID was approved without competitive bidding.

HIID was in a unique position in providing U.S. aid policy advice, because through a noncompetitive cooperative agreement, it received $40.4 million from USAID to undertake a number of activities in Russia. HIID was the main contractor that was also overseeing U.S. contractors' delivery of more than $285 million to Russian institutions and private companies. In 1996, the GAO was asked by Congress to investigate HIID activities in Russia and Ukraine and issued its report stressing that USAID's management and oversight of this contractor had been "lax" (GAO 1996b, 48).

After an investigation, an additional $17.4 million HIID was to receive was revoked, because this contractor had "abused the trust of the U.S. government by using personal relationships for private gain" (Robbins and Leisman 1997).

The privatization program in Russia lent itself to widespread corruption that benefitted only the few, particularly those in key positions of power or who had ties to those with inside information. Aid promoted a particular group of people with their own agenda. Rather than generating competition by transforming state monopolies to private enterprises, it turned them into lucrative private monopolies acquired by few individuals. By the time USAID and other Western donors brought their aid programs under closer scrutiny, much of the aid money had been misappropriated.

Other problems with aid that have been widely discussed in the literature include the lack of coordination on the part of donor agencies, unsuitable aid programs, poor evaluation of aid projects, and their limited measurable contribution to reducing extreme poverty (Wood 1986, 1996; Hirschman 1967; Raffer and Singer 1996).

It is widely assumed that development aid can accelerate the pace of economic development and poverty reduction. However, Stokke (1996) and Riddell (1996) contend that the new approach to development assistance, which relies more on market forces, has not reduced, alleviated, or eliminated poverty and deprivation. In fact, the problems of development have become even more pressing. As Riddell (1996) puts it, "solutions are now seen to be in the hands of the poor themselves" (198).

Over the years, USAID has been hampered in its efforts to achieve its objectives by persistent management problems and political difficulties. The General Accounting Office, which audits USAID's foreign assistance programs, has identified, analyzed, and reported many of the problems faced by the agency. The GAO in 1991 (GAO 1991a,b) raised concerns about USAID's lack of effective oversight of contracts. The expected benefits of decreased implementation costs, reduced administrative costs, increased institution building, and growth of private enterprise abroad were not realized. Moreover, the GAO (1990; 1992e) has stressed that USAID needs to strengthen its management practices by establishing better built-in implementation and evaluation capabilities. Academic observers such as Rondinelli (1987) and Ruttan (1996) have also suggested that USAID has long needed a more effective program administration.

Without any solid constituency to support it, USAID has been subject to much controversy. In its thirty five years of existence, USAID has been examined by more commissions and independent study groups than any other government agency (Ruttan 1996). A Congressional Task Force on Foreign Assistance in the late 1980s claimed that the assistance program had been ineffective and unfocused, and had failed to reflect the changing nature of the international economy (Ruttan1996). Even former USAID Administrator Alan Woods admitted in his report that the agency suffered from a lack of direction (Woods 1989).

What has not been fully examined in the controversy over foreign assistance is the role of special interests that influence the direction of foreign aid. Strong domestic support for certain countries can translate into aid packages, such as large aid packages for Israel or post Cold-War Eastern Europe. That means fewer aid resources to Africa, for example, which has no powerful domestic constituency. Private for-profit contractors form a sector that has more than doubled in the last decade (GAO 1995a, 10), and are now major actors in international development; they are in a position to influence policy. Their interests are in generating and maintaining profitable contracts. This is not inherently antithetical to effective development—the whole premise of privatization is that it will provide more efficient, effective services. An effective program will help domestic agencies and encourage and nurture foreign development, which in turn will benefit the domestic economy. However, some researchers have expressed concern that the creation of a system that stresses U.S. contractors may work against the growth of strong, self-sufficient organizations and businesses in LDCs (GAO 1992b,c; Raffer and Singer 1996; Rondinelli 1987; Tarnoff and Nowels 1994).

SCOPE OF U.S. DEVELOPMENT AID

Since foreign aid is an instrument of U.S. foreign policy, much of the money provided is concentrated in a few countries that best serve the foreign policy goals of the United States. Only a small fraction of U.S. aid benefits the poorest regions, and the existing programs do not always try to satisfy crucial development needs.[2] Moreover, since aid is often conditional, this undermines the sovereignty of recipients and reflects selected priority concerns of the donor. In the case of the United States, these concerns are mainly political, economic, and strategic in nature. The goals of aid are far reaching, even if they are conflicting at times. These include promoting private capital development, securing markets for U.S. goods, rewarding allies for strategic purposes, and providing humanitarian relief when disaster strikes. Under the existing system, geopolitical issues and economic concerns have replaced the bipolar Cold War rivalry. Approximately less than half of U.S. foreign aid is allocated to be channeled through USAID. In FY1998, $6.107 billion was appropriated to USAID ($6.974 actually administered) of a total budget of $13.15 billion for Foreign Operations appropriations or one-seventh of 1 percent of the total government's budget. Of this amount, bilateral development assistance programs managed by USAID in FY1999 account for only 19.4 percent of the total foreign aid appropriated, food aid is only 3.7 percent, and humanitarian aid is 8.4 percent. The other half is distributed in the form of military aid (25.3 percent) and security related economic aid (30.9 percent), multilateral aid (12.3 percent), as well as aid for the promotion of U.S. exports,[3] and other forms of nondevelopment aid. Figure 4.1

Figure 4.1
Program Composition of Aid, 1999

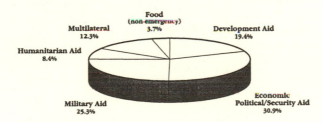

Economic/political security aid includes Middle East, Eastern Europe, and the fomer Soviet Union.
Source: House and Senate Appropriations Committee and CRS calculations. Taken from Curt Tarnoff and Larry Nowels, *Foreign Aid: An Introductory Overview of U.S. Programs and Policy*, 6 November, 1998.

Table 4.2
Regional Allocation of U.S. Bilateral Foreign Aid

(US$ millions, %)

REGION	1955	1965	1975	1985	1995
Africa	48.56	196.85	294.48	894.52	873.72
	(1%)	(5%)	(6%)	(11%)	(12%)
Asia	2622.61	2049.24	2503.08	1138.48	436.86
	(54%)	(52%)	(51%)	(14%)	(6%)
Europe*/NIS	1748.41	511.81	245.40	1138.48	1310.58
	(36%)	(13%)	(5%)	(14%)	(18%)
Latin America	145.70	787.40	539.88	1219.80	655.89
	(3%)	(20%)	(11%)	(15%)	(9%)
Middle East	291.40	393.70	1325.16	3659.40	4004.55
	(6%)	(10%)	(27%)	(45%)	(55%)

*Europe refers to Western, Eastern and Central. NIS are the Newly Independent States of the former Soviet Union.
Source: based on data from USAID, *U.S. Overseas Loans and Grants. Obligations and Loan Authorizations, 1946-1995, (1996).* Office of the Budget, Bureau of Management of USAID (1997).

shows this distribution, from which one can deduce that only a small part of the total foreign aid budget is allocated to sustainable development programs.

Many authors (Griffin 1991; Hook 1995; Tarnoff and Nowels 1996; Sexton and Decker 1992) have stressed that the geographical distribution of U.S. development assistance has been above all to countries serving the geopolitical and security concerns of the day, and not to the countries that are in greatest need. This political rationale for U.S. foreign assistance is illustrated in Table 4.2, which shows the regional concentration profile and country distribution of aid resources for the last fifty years in the areas where the United States had specific interests over time.

The direction and allocation of U.S. aid has changed in the last five decades, depending on who was in office and which party had control of Congress. Table 4.3 depicts how U.S. foreign aid is concentrated in just a few countries. In FY1997, the top ten recipients accounted for 70 percent of bilateral aid to individual countries. Israel and Egypt account for more than half. Second in importance were the countries of the former Soviet Union and Central and Eastern Europe. In 1997, aid to this region constituted almost 17 percent of the bilateral aid budget, whereas the entire continent of Africa received just 12 percent.

Table 4.3
Leading Recipients of U.S. Foreign Aid, FY 1997

Israel	$3000
Egypt	$2116
Bosnia	$286
Ukraine	$229
Jordan	$193
Russia	$134
Georgia	$93
Armenia	$88
West Bank/Gaza	$85
Haiti	$71

Source: USAID.

Between 1946 and 1952, 82 percent of U.S. bilateral assistance went to Europe. In the 1950s and 1960s, the focus of U.S. spending shifted from Europe to Asia, particularly South Korea, Taiwan, and later, South Vietnam. During these two decades that region received about half of U.S. assistance. Funding priorities shifted from Asia to the Middle East in the mid-1970s after South Vietnam fell to the North Vietnamese. In 1979, the Camp David accords were signed between Israel and Egypt, promoting assistance programs in both countries. Since 1979 these two countries have received between one-third and one-half of the allocation of U.S. bilateral net disbursement (DAC 1998). According to Zimmerman (1993), aid to Egypt and Israel has been used to buttress U.S. political and strategic objectives, rather than for development. Latin America during the 1980s and 1990s received 13 percent of U.S. assistance; Africa, where the largest number of least developed countries are concentrated, has been a low priority, receiving slightly more than 10 percent in the 1990s.

As was pointed out earlier, the volume of U.S. official development assistance (ODA) has been declining. By the mid-1990s it was only half of what it had been a decade before. By DAC standards, assistance provided to Sub-Saharan Africa has always been small, and with the closing of many USAID country missions, the impact of U.S. development assistance is below that of other donor countries such as France and Germany. One author has noted that "by 1975, China had aid programs in more African countries than did the United States" (Brautingam 1998, 4). Near the very end of the millennium, some ninety nine countries had received Chinese aid. Similarly, Haugaard (1997) reports that U.S. aid levels to Latin America in 1997 were one-third of what they were in 1990.

As the former Soviet Union and Eastern Europe underwent economic transformation in the 1990s, the emphasis of U.S. assistance shifted back to Europe and the Middle East. In the post-Cold War era competition for U.S. assistance increased with the incorporation of the former socialist countries, thus reorienting resources and diverting personnel from what was known as the "Third World" to the "Second World." Following the collapse of the Soviet model of communism, the United States offered more optimism than substance or experience. Consistent with the objectives of U.S. foreign assistance, the priority of this aid was intended for economic

"reform" and to foster the privatization drive of state-owned enterprises or what is known as private sector development. Other areas
such as public administration, health, and local governance were
given less attention. However, some of the aid provided was
through personal contacts, granted to certain groups, or lent to
small businesses. Wedel (1998a,b), who has followed this trend,
notes that after seven years of U.S. and other Western aid, Russia
finds itself worse off economically. Part of the problem was that
USAID was easily persuaded to hand over millions of dollars for projects that were never adequately monitored, were poorly managed,
and had little oversight.

Figure 4.2, in the form of a pie chart for FY1997, illustrates the
geographic regional distribution of American aid. The chart shows
that the LDCs of Africa, Asia, and Latin America accounted for 24.5
percent of U.S. assistance, whereas Europe (Western as well as
Central and Eastern, and the NIS) received 17.8 percent and the
Middle East 57.7 percent. It is evident from the chart that the
decline of aid allocated to LDCs of Africa, Asia, and Latin America
has been supplanted by the creation of aid programs to Eastern and
Central Europe, including Russia and the NIS.

Figure 4.2
Regional Allocation of U.S. Foreign Aid, FY 1997

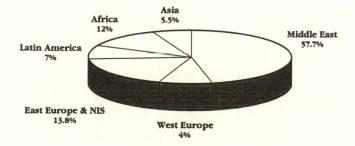

Source: USAID, *Congressional Presentation Summary Tables, FY 1997* (July 1996).

For most of the post-World War II period, the United States was the main provider of assistance. Even in 1968, the United States, accounted for half of the total dollar value of this aid. In 1995, the United States represented only 13 percent of total donor bilateral disbursements. While U.S. assistance was declining, other industrialized countries took the lead. According to one report, if U.S. aid to Israel and Egypt is excluded, "the United States spends less on development assistance than Denmark" (Mazur and Sechler 1997, 11). By 1995, the United States had fallen behind Japan, France, and Germany in the absolute level of assistance and ranked last among the twenty one OECD donors in terms of percentage of GNP (see

Figure 4.3
Foreign Aid by Donors as Percentage of GNP, 1995

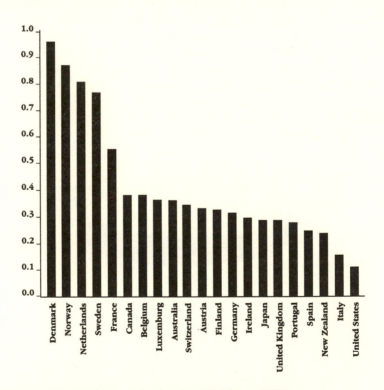

Source: OECD, *Development Cooperation 1996 Report* (1997).

Figure 4.3). By this relative measure the United States has become the least-generous official provider of aid of the industrialized countries of the OECD. In fact, during the second half of the 1990s, the U.S. ratio of ODA to GNP was at its lowest since 1950 (less than one-tenth of 1 percent).

Finally, as privatization of social services has increased in LDCs because of the policies of multilateral financial institutions demanding structural adjustment, conditionality of aid has also increased. Aid is made to be conditional on the success of the LDC governments in cutting public spending, introducing free market policies, and freeing up their domestic economy for foreign investment (Raffer and Singer 1996; Crawford 1997). As a result, private capital flows to LDCs have increased substantially to about three times global aid flows (O'Hanlon and Graham 1997). But increased direct foreign investment is not a substitute for aid. The *World Development Report 1997* (World Bank 1997) figures show that foreign direct investment has been significant, but only in a select group of countries with sizeable markets (e.g., China, Brazil, Mexico). The world's poorest countries (many of which are in Africa) have hardly been part of the globalization phenomenon (Cason 1997; Kimaru 1996).

NOTES

1. In the mid-1980s, the United Nations Development Programme (UNDP) set up the NATCAP (National Technical Cooperation and Assistance Programme) so that recipient governments could do national technical cooperation assessments outlining the policies and pinpointing the problems. To date the system has been used in some thirty African countries as well as a handful of other countries in other regions. See Berg (1993) and UNDP (1989).

2. According to USAID estimates, "The 50 poorest countries, home to one-fifth of the world's population, now account for 2 percent of the global income—and this share is decreasing." See *The USAID Fact Sheet*, 1998, p. 4.

3. Since broad-based economic growth in LDCs is one of the strategic goals of U.S. development assistance, USAID is involved in the promotion of trade policy under the Commodity Import Programs. Such programs makes dollars available to the assisted country on a loan or grant basis to pay for imports from the United States. These imports include agricultural goods,

construction and transportation equipment, chemicals, raw materials, finished products, and foodstuffs.

5

Methods of Awarding Contracts and Types of Contracts

Government contracting is a complex and highly regulated process. This chapter details the rules that govern contracting and lays out the mechanics of procurement.

The framework in which USAID works is that which regulates all government agencies. The variations within that framework and the path USAID has chosen in terms of types of contracts used and relationships with contractors will be more clear within the broad context of this explanation of government contracting.

PHASES OF CONTRACTING AND ADMINISTRATION OF CONTRACTS

The government procurement process, in general, works in sequential phases. These are the planning, solicitation, and administration of the contract. Each phase has several steps. As figure 5.1 shows, the agency must first establish its procurement needs, which depend on its program requirement and organizational mission. The budget for these programs must be there. Then the procurement method must be determined. The solicitation to prospective contractors is then issued requesting the submission of offers or of information. The solicitation states the factors that will be considered in evaluating proposals. The evaluation and selection is then made to determine the merits of an offer and the offeror's ability to accomplish a prospective contract. The contract is awarded to the offeror providing "best value" to government. This determination is made on the basis of price or cost and non-cost factors such as technical excellence, management capabilities, and professional

Figure 5.1
Phases of Contracting

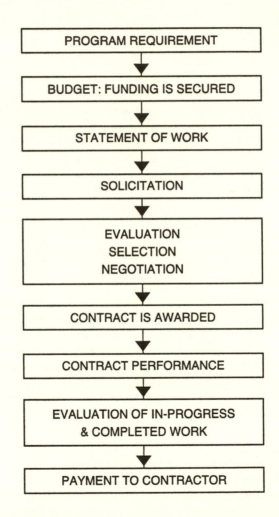

PROGRAM REQUIREMENT

BUDGET: FUNDING IS SECURED

STATEMENT OF WORK

SOLICITATION

EVALUATION
SELECTION
NEGOTIATION

CONTRACT IS AWARDED

CONTRACT PERFORMANCE

EVALUATION OF IN-PROGRESS
& COMPLETED WORK

PAYMENT TO CONTRACTOR

experience. Past performance is also now an evaluation in all competitive procurement acquisitions (FAR 15.304).

The administrative activity of the contract runs from the time of the award to contract close-out. Government representatives and contractors must show compliance with the terms and conditions of the contract, which includes monitoring contractor progress, processing payments, making necessary changes or solving problems that arise along the way, and evaluating the performance upon completion of the contract (Nash, Schooner, and O'Brien 1998).

The requirements and directives governing the acquisition of supplies or services for the government are established in the Federal Acquisition Regulation (FAR). This document contains the policies and procedures that govern the acquisition activity of all federal agencies. In it, the government grants full responsibility to the contracting officer (CO), who executes the government procurement action and has the authority to sign contracts. The program officials have primary responsibilities for the steps during the planning phase, and contracting officials have responsibilities in the formation and administration of the contract. The contracting officer, who is the buyer or negotiator, assumes responsibility once the technical specialists have defined the specifications and delivery requirements and any other pertinent information of the procurement. The responsibility of the contracting officer is to ensure that the award is made in the best interest of the government. In the post award or contract administration phase, the contracting officer can delegate some contract administration authority to program officers. The program officer who is delegated authority by the CO is referred to as the contracting officer technical representative, or COTR. The COTR then has authority to handle some of the technical aspects of contract administration.

It is in this phase, after the award has been made, that USAID has the most problems, such as the conflict between the CO and the technical officers who have been named COTRs. The FAR gives only general guidance of the use of program or technical officers in contract administration. Each government agency has to work out its supplementary FAR guidance—in the case of USAID, the AID Acquisition Regulation (AIDAR)—regarding the delegation of contracting officer authority to technical officers in the post-award phase.[1] Unfortunately, USAID has not done a good job of defining the role of the COTR and the process of delegating authority.

The main medium through which government agencies make contracting opportunities known is through the *Commerce Business Daily* (CBD), published every business day of the year by the Department of Commerce. Anyone who does business with the U.S. government subscribes to this publication. Solicitations are announced in it after a requirement has been defined by the government agency.

The section immediately following will discuss the difference between invitations for bids (IFBs) and requests for proposals (RFPs), and the subsequent paragraphs will discuss fixed-price and cost-reimbursement contracts.

If the government wishes to purchase an item and provides detailed specifications, an IFB would normally be used to solicit the bids. When the government knows exactly what it wants and the quantity it wants to buy, the contract would be a fixed-price type of contract. Fixed-price is essentially the bidding price, not subject to adjustment.[2] On the other hand, if the government were requesting a special purpose item or service, an RFP might be issued to solicit proposals. There are many instances in which the agency asks the contractor to estimate the probable costs and base a fixed fee on those probable costs. This procedure is common at USAID mainly because of the uncertainty in an overseas environment. USAID also uses the RFP, even though it is a more difficult and time consuming contracting procedure. The contract used is often cost-reimbursement, in which the government guarantees to pay all reasonable costs plus some negotiated fixed fee or profit (Cibinic and Nash 1993, 1998).

NEGOTIATED VERSUS NON-NEGOTIATED CONTRACTS

The federal government employs two different methods for procuring goods and services: sealed bidding and negotiated procurement (Holtz 1979). The former is a method of contracting that employs competitive sealed bids that are awarded to the lowest responsible bidder. The latter, contract by negotiation, is a method that makes use of discussions and negotiations to reach a contractual agreement (Nash and Cibinic 1993).

Sealed bidding is a competitive method of contracting and is generally perceived as impartial in the way of obtaining competitive bids. Sealed bidding anticipates adequate price competition because without it there is no assurance that the price of the lowest bidder will be fair and reasonable. As mentioned above, the contract type in a sealed-bid acquisition is the firm fixed-price type.

Under the fixed-price type of contract maximum risk and responsibility is borne by the contractor, who assumes full responsibility for profits or losses. By bidding on the solicitation, the contractor agrees to the firm fixed price contract type at inception (Management Concepts 1990).

This type of contracting is suitable for use in acquisitions with definite specifications. It is particularly suitable in the purchase of standard or modified commercial items on which adequate information on cost is available.

Sealed bidding involves the following process: The first step in an acquisition is to prepare an IFB. Invitations for bids must describe the contractual requirements of the government (such as delivery schedule, clauses, and specialized requirements). The second step is publicizing the IFBs, which must be advertised in the *Commerce Business Daily* and distributed to the prospective bidders, allowing sufficient time (at least thirty days in most cases) to enable prospective bidders to prepare and submit bids. Third, prospective contractors submit sealed bids to be opened at a time and place set for the public opening of bids. Fourth, bids are evaluated by the contracting officer, who determines whether each bidder's offer is responsive to the requirements. Finally, after bids are publicly opened, the award is made to the bidder whose bid conforms to the essential provisions of the IFB and whose bid is most advantageous to the government, based on price and other price-related factors (Cibinic and Nash 1993).

Procurement by negotiation is a method of government procurement that is more flexible than sealed bidding. Negotiation leads to discussion of deficiencies with the offeror and provides the offeror the opportunity to revise its offer. Negotiation then leads to selection. Under negotiation, estimated costs must be supported by evidence of reasonable prices as deemed necessary by the contracting officer. Attention is given to various factors of procurement, such as technical excellence, management capability, prior experience, cost factors, consideration of delivery requirements, and now, the firm's past performance (Holtz 1979; Nash and Cibinic 1993; Riemer 1968). The changes were made in 1995 and reiterated in the FAR rewrite (FAR 15.304 (c) (2).

The steps in negotiation as a procurement process are as follows: First, the requirement is identified. The technical office prepares the RFP, describing the requirements established by the government. Second, the RFP must be briefly synopsized in the *Commerce Business Daily*. It must contain information required by the FAR, and closing date for submitting proposals is announced with anticipated issuance date. RFPs are used to communicate government requirements to prospective contractors and to solicit proposals from them. Third is the solicitation phase, where the proposal is received in response to the RFP by prospective contractors and reviewed. It must contain whatever is required in the RFP: a technical proposal on how to perform the contract based on the statement of work, cost estimates, technical details (such as a plan for staffing, estimate of tasks, functions, materials, man-hours, schedules), and information about the firm's experience (Nash and Cibinic 1993).

Solicitations contain the information necessary to enable prospective contractors to prepare proposals. The RFP must set forth the non-cost evaluation criteria on which proposals will be evaluated, the relative importance or weight attached to them, and their relationship to price (Holtz 1979). Offerors are made aware of all relevant award factors and their relative merit. This will be used by the contracting officer, with the assistance of the technical team, in determining which offers are within a "competitive range." That is, is the contracting firm technically qualified and competitive in price? The contracting officer then holds discussions with those offerors who are in the competitive range.

Once proposals are received, the technical evaluation team assesses, based on stated selection criteria, for clarification and deficiencies. All potential recipients are now subject to past-performance scrutiny. Then the contract negotiator does the cost analysis to obtain "reasonableness" of cost (with input from the technical team). There is a comparison of the business reputation, capabilities, and responsibility of the firm that submits a proposal. Weaknesses and strengths of the proposal are discussed. Selection of offerors who are in the competitive range and have a reasonable chance of being awarded a contract is determined. Those who make the competitive range are invited to make a "best and final" offer on which the final selection will be made. Then final offers are made based on the negotiated points. Once all necessary clearances have been obtained, award is made.

The advantages of sealed bidding to the government could be summarized as follows:

1. All suppliers regardless of size compete.
2. The process lessens considerably the possibility of favoritism and collusion.
3. Competition is stimulated, enabling the government to secure the best possible price.
4. The process minimizes arbitrary selection of contracts.
5. The process is especially efficient in the purchase of very specific items (orders).
6. There is a minimum amount of administration to supervise.

The disadvantages of sealed bidding could be listed as follows:

1. The system is not flexible enough and requires strict adherence to rules and regulations
2. It is impractical for small procurement
3. If the IFB is voluminous and overly detailed, it may deter small firms from entering the competition
4. Awarding the contract to the lowest bidder (without properly calculating the vendor's responsibility) could result in the firm engaging in low balling, which occurs when the firm intentionally bids excessively low just to get the contract.
5. If specifications are not adequate, results could be unsatisfactory, as many bidders offer inferior product that technically meets specifications.

Advantages of negotiation could be listed as follows:

1. Some type of work lends itself to negotiation because precise specifications are rarely available
2. Negotiation is better in cases of immediate need where sources of supply are a critical factor

The disadvantages of negotiated contracts are:

1. Subjectivity and judgment are involved in decisions of a negotiated procurement.
2. Administration of these types of contracts is more costly.
3. It involves more documentation and it takes more time.

SELECTION OF CONTRACT TYPE

The selection of the type of contract is the responsibility of the Contracting Officer. It is the CO who decides the type of contract to be specified in the solicitation. Each type of contract establishes a different relationship between the contractor and the government. Essentially, contracts vary according to the degree of responsibility assumed by the contractor for the cost performance and the amount of profit incentive offered to the contractor (Baker et al. 1993).

There are more than a dozen types of contracts listed in the FAR, part 16, ranging from fixed-price to cost-plus. In the former, the contractor has full responsibility for the cost performance and resulting profit (or losses). In the latter, the contractor has minimal responsibility for the cost performance and the profit is fixed. In between are incentive contracts in which performance and profit (or fee) are tailored to the uncertainties involved (MacManus 1992; Management Concepts 1990).

In fixed-price contracts, the contractor guarantees performance as a condition for being paid. Cost reimbursement, on the other hand, merely provides for the contractor to use its best efforts as a condition for being paid all allowable costs up to a ceiling plus a fee. In cost-reimbursement, the contract will specify an estimated amount which cannot be exceeded, but the amount can increase at the discretion of the contracting officer.

Important factors considered in selecting the type of contract to be awarded have to do with uncertainties and risks involved as well as financial implications (Management Concepts 1990; Nagle 1990). Under the fixed-price type of contract, the contractor assumes all the risks. In the other types of contracts, the government bears a portion or most of the risk of cost control. The financial implications have to do with tracking all costs, estimating these costs, and the payment process that would determine what type of contract to select.

In selecting and negotiating a contract, the contracting officer must consider the following factors:

Price competition. It is important when price is a significant element in the source selection. There is price competition if an adequate number (more than one) of vendors is competing (MacManus 1992; Nash, Schooner, O'Brien 1998).

Price analysis. This involves the comparison of the proposed price with other prices offered, or with current or recent contract prices for similar goods and services.

Cost analysis. This is the review and evaluation of the cost estimate contained in the contractor's proposal. It includes an estimate of the cost to perform the work. It is used to establish a basis for negotiating contract prices.

Type and complexity of the requirement. Standard types of goods and services can be accurately defined by the government. More complex procurement might involve a level of risk making it difficult to estimate cost performance.

Length of time to complete task. The longer the duration of work, the more uncertainties might emerge.

Contractor's technical capability. Personnel must have specialized knowledge, skills, and the technical experience to be awarded the contract.

TYPES OF CONTRACTS

Contract type is determined by what the government is buying (goods or services), the procurement method (either sealed bidding or negotiated procurement), dollar amount of the contract, and method of payment (fixed price or cost reimbursement) it intends to use. The type of contract can change the risks and responsibilities of the parties. If the government selects an inappropriate type of contract, the costs incurred by the government increase.

The two broad categories of contracts are fixed-price and cost-reimbursement. Within these basic types, there are a number of other specific types. Under fixed-price there are firm fixed-price contracts, fixed-price incentive contracts, fixed-price with economic adjustments, and others. Cost-reimbursement includes cost-plus term, cost-plus completion, cost-plus fixed-fee, and cost-plus award-fee. For our purposes we are separating all these categories into three types: fixed-fee, cost-plus fixed-fee, and incentive-type contracts (both award and incentive types). Other types of contracts defined later, such as time and materials and indefinite quantity contracts, are in some respects similar to fixed-price-type contracts.

Fixed-Price Contracts

Fixed-price contracts are based on an agreed-upon unit cost for a good or service. A fixed price contract provides a firm price that is established in the proposal. Fixed-price contracts are used when the specifications are definite and precise particularly for commercial items. This type of contract imposes 100 percent of the risk on the contractor. For instance, if USAID is requesting a delivery of fifty computers to South Africa, a fixed type contract is most appropriate.

A fixed-price contract is suitable in acquisitions that have a definite design or when the cost or pricing information is available for performance specifications. It is also suitable when there is adequate competition, and uncertainties involved in contract performance can be identified.

From the point of view of the government, the fixed-price type of contract is preferable because it imposes the greatest risk on the contractor. The contractor has the greatest incentive to control cost and perform efficiently, and the government has minimal administrative burden. For instance, a contractor agrees to perform at a set price, say $1,000 per item. However, if the contractor has miscalculated and the item ends up costing $1,500, it must suffer a loss. Conversely, if the contractor can produce an acceptable product at $500 per item, it has earned a 100 percent profit. A firm fixed-price contract is best used when the risk involved is minimal or can be predicted with a fair amount of certainty.

Fixed-price contracts with economic price adjustment are used when price adjustment provisions are necessary to protect the government and the contractor against significant economic fluctuations that can change the established prices. Fixed-price contracts with economic price adjustment are common in situations of high inflation or market volatility. Under such conditions, contractors are reluctant to lock themselves into firm fixed-price contracts without allowing for provision for price increases. To accommodate this, the government uses economic adjustment clauses that account for price changes for labor or materials. The use of this type of contract reduces the contractor's risk because the contractor is afforded protection.

Under fixed-price contracts, payments by the government are directly tied to the value of the work actually accomplished on the value of services delivered. If the contractor fails to perform the government may withhold payments and eventually terminate the contract for default. The government pays only for the predetermined value of the benefit delivered or received from the contractor.

Cost-Reimbursement Contracts

Cost-reimbursement contracts are used when the requirements have uncertainties. These contracts are negotiated to come to agreement on what and how contractors are proposing to provide the service or supplies required by the government. Negotiations also try to clarify what is imprecise in the solicitation or simply to come to a mutual understanding. Once agreed upon, an estimate is made of the cost. These types of contracts establish an estimate of total cost for the purpose of obligating the funds and setting a ceiling that the contractor may exceed, but only with the approval of the contracting officer. The majority of USAID large multiyear contracts are cost-reimbursement.

Whereas in the fixed-price type of contract the contractor is not paid unless the service is performed (or product delivered) and accepted, in a cost-reimbursement contract the contractor is required to use its best efforts under the contract to be paid the allowable and reasonable costs. In the cost-reimbursement contract, the cost risk of performance is assumed mainly by the government. According to one source, "to compensate for this risk, the government must monitor contractor performance to assure that it receives the product or service it is paying for" (Management Concepts 1994, 5-1).

FAR 16.301-2 stresses that cost-reimbursement type of con-

tracts are suitable when the cost of performance cannot be estimated with reasonable accuracy to preclude the use of fixed-price
contracts. Cost-reimbursement contracts require that the cost
accounting of the contractor is adequate, that the government can
monitor the contractor to assure efficient methods and effective
costs are used, and that this type of contract is likely to be less costly than any other type. This type of contract is particularly useful
for acquisitions exceeding $100,000.

Under the cost-reimbursement contract, the government can
increase the stated amount of the award but only after it is negotiated for cost overruns or additional work. Allowable costs include
both direct and indirect costs. Some contracts require a fee.
Statutory limitations have been established on the maximum
amount of the fee. The fee may vary depending on the contract,
which often has to do with contractor effort, the degree of risk associated with the contract, and cost contract and past performance of
the contractor. The government also imposes ceilings on this type
of contract because of the number of cost overruns that can occur.
The two most commonly used types of ceilings incorporated into
the contract are on overall cost and ceilings on overhead (Cibinic
and Nash 1993).

For the purposes of this book, the discussion centers on the
four main types of cost-reimbursement contracts: cost-plus fixed-fee
(term and completion), cost-plus award-fee, and cost-plus incentive-
fee.

Cost-plus fixed-fee (CPFF) is a type of contract that provides for
reimbursement of all allowable estimated costs and for the payment
of a negotiated fee to the contractor. The fee, which is a fixed
amount of the profit, does not vary with the actual cost but may be
adjusted when there are changes in the work to be performed.
Sometimes contractors are often willing to agree to a lower cost
estimate to be awarded the contract.

The cost-plus fixed-fee contract is the most widely used
contract type in cost reimbursement. It is suitable for use when
it is an exploratory or preliminary study; or when the contract is
for work where the level of effort required to complete the
work is unknown. A question raised here, and to which I come
back later, is: why does USAID continue to use CPFF for projects
where it has a great deal of experience having implemented

them in several countries?

This type of contract requires the contractor to complete and deliver the specified end-product as condition for payment of the entire fee established for the work. The fixed fee is payable at the expiration of the agreed period of time and after the work has been considered satisfactory to the government. The CPFF comes in two basic forms: completion or term. The former is one that describes the scope of the work to be done with a definite goal or target to be completed and delivered. The latter describes the scope of work to be done in general terms and obligates the contractor to devote a specified level of effort for a stated period of time. Many of the contracts awarded by USAID are CPFF-term or "level of effort" contracts.

According to Management Concepts (1990), "the cost-plus fixed-fee type of contract is the least desirable contract from the government's viewpoint based on cost risk performance. Since the fixed fee does not vary in relationship to the contractor's ability to control costs, the CPFF contract provides minimal incentive to the contractor for effective management of costs." (5-12). Given the amount of risk involved because of cost overruns, the government must assume a significant administrative burden to ensure that the contractor employs efficient and cost-effective methods.

For illustrative purposes, the CPFF works as follows: The contractor estimates that it would take one year to complete the project. This would involve $35,000 in labor costs plus $25,000 of other direct costs, totaling $60,000. The contractor requests a fee of 8 percent, or $4,800. If the government accepts this contract, the contractor will be paid for his actual costs plus $4,800 profit or fee. A ceiling cost might be set at $70,000 or more if there are additional cost overruns.

Cost-plus award-fee (CPAF) is a cost-reimbursement type of contract, but it is herewith considered an incentive-type contract consisting of the base fee and an award fee that is paid to the contractor for performing the work, periodically, based on the government's evaluation of his performance. The base amount is fixed at the inception of the contract. The award fee is based on a subjective evaluation by the contracting officer for awarding the contractor for good performance. The award fee mechanism provides a basic financial motivation for the contractor's performance in terms of quality, timeliness, and cost-effectiveness (FAR 16.404-2[a]). According to Holtz (1979), "if the contractor has saved the government money by bringing the product well under the original estimated cost or if he has delivered other benefits, he will get a generous award fee" (63).

Although the quote from Holtz might seem dated, CPAF contracts can produce a better product or service. A major advantage of CPAF contracts is that there is greater communication among the parties. As the work proceeds, the government provides detailed evaluation of contractor performance. However, CPAF contracts require more administrative effort on the part of the government to conduct performance evaluations and in processing award decisions.

From the point of view of the government, CPAF contracts differ substantially from the CPFF where the attitude is essentially, if you do the work we will give you so much. In CPAF, the award fee is based on the quality of the performance. The amount received by the contractor provides a motivation for excellence and cost-effective management. The determination to pay the award fee above the base fee is made unilaterally by the government and is not subject to dispute (Cibinic and Nash, 1998).

According to USAID (1997), experience has confirmed that in many procurements of support services, the award fee approach can provide contractor motivation, flexibility, improved management, and more fluid communication. The overall quality of contractor performance could be enhanced with a periodic award-fee evaluation. An award-fee type of contract can more effectively manage the contract effort to reflect any changes that might occur during performance.

Cost-plus incentive-fee (CPIF) is a cost-reimbursement type contract that provides for a fee that is adjusted by a formula based on the relationship of total allowable costs to total target costs. It is also a contract that gives the contractor higher profits for better performance or lower profits for bad performance in such areas as cost, delivery, and technical competence. A CPIF contract specifies a target cost and a target fee, a minimum and maximum fee, and a fee adjustment formula negotiated at the outset. When the work is completed, the fee payable to the contractor is determined in accordance with the formula. The increase or decrease in the fee is intended to provide an incentive to contractors in managing the contract effectively (Cibinic and Nash 1998).

CPIF contracts are used for research and development projects in which firm specification and adequate pricing information are not available. Incentive contracts are used not when the low bidder offers the best value, but rather when the technical competence of the contractor may be of greater significance and thus an incentive approach is desirable. An incentive contract is intended to provide a desirable profit motivation to the contractor (Riemer 1968). An element of incentive contracts is that the cost-sharing formula is negotiated and the government shares part of the risk. For example, if a 90/10 cost-sharing formula is negotiated, for every dollar saved, the government retains 90 cents, and the contractor's profit (or fee) will increase by 10 cents. In other words, the contractor looks at every dollar he spends as though 10 percent of it were his.

CPIF is different from CPFF in that the former uses profit motivation to provide the stimulus. As Riemer (1968) puts it, "CPFF has no real incentive, but in CPIF a contractor can increase his actual profit as well as his percentage of profit by doing a good job" (293).

For illustrative purposes, a CPIF works as follows: The target cost is $1,000,000, the target fee, $75,000, the maximum fee, $135,000, the minimum fee, $30,000, and there is a sharing formula of 85/15. Assuming that the final cost is $900,000, the contractor's target fee of $75,000 is increased by its share of the reduction in cost of $15,000 (15 percent of $100,000), and the government saves $85,000 (85 percent of $100,000), resulting in a total price of $990,000.

If the target cost is exceeded, and final costs are $1,200,000, the contractor's fee is reduced by its share of the increased cost of $30,000 (15% of $200,000). Thus the contractor fee is $45,000 and the final cost of the contract to the government is $1,245,000.

Other Variants

Time and materials (T&M). These are contracts in which the contractor is paid agreed-upon rates for labor and materials, plus some agreed-upon profit percentage. Labor hours are specified at fixed hourly rates that include wages, fringe benefits, overhead, administrative cost, and profit. The contract has a ceiling price that the contractor exceeds at his own risk.

Basic ordering agreement (BOA). This is not exactly a contract, but a written instrument of understanding. It is often referred to as a task order contract, under which the contractor provides services and materials at fixed rates. Under a BOA, the parties agree to general terms or conditions for future orders of supplies or services to be provided. The BOA contains terms and clauses specifying the conditions for invoicing, methods of delivery, and quantity.

Indefinite Quantity (IQC). These are common contracts now used by USAID, particularly in the transition economies of Central and Eastern Europe. The main features of IQCs are that daily rates are set for functional labor categories. The rate includes the salary cost or consulting fee of the individual performing the service, plus other costs such as benefits and per diem. They work as follows: USAID awards a delivery order for a project task. A delivery order represents an agreement between the agency and the contractor on what is going to be done, the level of effort involved, and the key personnel who will carry out the work. The contractor bills the agency at specified daily rates.

NOTES

1. AIDAR supplements the FAR and implements the procurement related aspects of the Foreign Assistance Act, Executive Order 11223.

2. There is also fixed-price with economic price adjustment clauses, which incorporate market variability considerations into price. A fixed-price contract with economic price adjustment provides a fixed price that can be adjusted upward or downward. It is used sometimes to protect the contractor and the government against economic fluctuations because of a volatile marketplace (in terms of materials and labor costs).

6

Performance-Based Contracting and Past Performance

PROCUREMENT REFORM IN THE CONTEXT OF REINVENTING GOVERNMENT

For several years the General Accounting Office (GAO) has been documenting poor performance in the purchase of services in the government. The GAO and other government reports, particularly in the case of USAID, stress that service contracts have poorly defined work statements, have contract administration problems that need to be addressed, and have performed inefficiently (GAO 1992b; 1992c; OMB-AID Swat Team 1992).

In 1993, the federal government began implementing a variety of outcome/results-driven performance management strategies in its various agencies, with the goal of improving program performance. Two of these initiatives are performance-based contracting (PBC) and past performance (PP). The purpose of this chapter is to define performance-based contracting as a new guiding principle in service contracting, examine how this fits in with USAID's objectives, and assess what its accomplishments have been. The second part of the chapter examines the reform initiatives undertaken at USAID, and the third and last section discusses the use of past performance information to improve program results.

The Clinton administration has made a concerted effort to reform the federal procurement system. Legislation since 1994 has removed some of the burdens of government contracting. One of the keystones of procurement reform has been revisions of the Federal Acquisition Regulation (FAR), the blueprint for federal contracting procedures, and the adoption of the PBC and PP initiatives.

The reform in procurement process has been implemented with the intention of making a transition from prescriptive rules to guiding principles (von Opstal 1995). The reform essentially was aimed at a stronger contract administration by eliminating redundant paperwork, pushing for greater clarity in solicitation, and fostering increased competition (USAID 1994).

According to the definition provided by the FAR 37.101, "performance-based contracting means structuring all aspects of an acquisition around the purpose of the work to be performed as opposed to either the manner by which the work is to be performed and on broad and imprecise statements of work." This means defining the requirements in terms of objective and measurable output, rather than describing how to do it. USAID formerly emphasized how the work was to be done in the statement of work (SOW) of the request for proposal (RFP). The contractor is no longer told how to go about doing what he or she has been hired to do, but what is expected of him or her is to deliver results. The steps taken in the process are up to the contractor, not USAID.

Performance-based contracting is an initiative that was proposed to improve government administration in procurement. It is part of and consistent with the "reinventing government" movement, which proposes an agenda for procurement reform. The main objective of PBC is streamlining procurement as a way of obtaining better results. More specifically, performance-based contracting is an effort to try to improve contractor performance by using measurable performance standards, managing contracts more efficiently, and fostering best-value selection. The federal government spends about $100 billion annually on contracts for services; it is now trying to set minimum standards for contractors to achieve results.

The benefits of performance-based contracting, as articulated by the government, are to encourage more competition through better proposals, to establish a new basis for evaluating contractor performance, to enhance monitoring and evaluation, and to increase contractor oversight (National Performance Review 1993a,b).

The concept of PBC can be traced to Office of Federal Procurement Policy (OFPP) Policy Letter 91-2 (1991), which emphasized the use of performance requirements and quality standards in contracting (OMB 1991). The new approach is essentially a method whereby the work to be performed is described in terms of results rather than by inputs or level of effort. However, implementation of such policy in most government agencies was limited, at best, because of other priorities.

The policy provided that government agencies use PBC methods to the *maximum* extent possible when acquiring services, and carefully select acquisition and contract administration strategies and methods that best accommodate the requirements. OFPP Policy Letter 92-1 (1992) provided guidance to agencies in contracting for services. Reviews by the Office of Management and Budget (OMB) stressed that common procurement management problems needed to be addressed.

At the 103rd Congress, the legislative branch passed the Government Performance and Results Act of 1993. The act provides for the establishment of strategic planning and performance measurement in the federal government. Some of its main points were: to institute program performance reform, improve federal program effectiveness and program accountability, help federal managers improve service delivery, and improve internal management of the federal government (Atlantic Management Center 1997). Another act that followed was the Federal Acquisition Streamlining Act of 1994, which was also intended to reduce the burden of doing business with the federal government.

As a follow-up to the President's Management Council meeting in 1993 and the OMB Director's Memorandum, Vice President Al Gore publicly launched the government initiative to "reinvent government," called the National Performance Review (NPR). The NPR report acknowledged that the system had excessive rules and regulations that placed a heavy burden on the government to deliver services. It admits that the procurement system was complex, excessively bureaucratic, and increasingly less productive (NPR 1993b). NPR's recommendations for procurement focused on the need to revamp the procurement process, to reduce unneeded burdens and bureaucratic procedures, to emphasize customer needs, and to foster competition, excellence in vendor performance, and best-value procurement.

The new initiative on PBC encourages an increased use of fixed price and incentive type of contracts to encourage optimal performance. Under the new approach, firm fixed-price contracts are considered appropriate for services that can be objectively defined in the solicitation and for which risk of performance is manageable. "For such acquisitions, performance-based statement of work, measurable performance standards and surveillance plans are ideally suitable. The contractor is motivated to find improved methods of performance in order to increase its profits" (AMC 1997, appendix 1, p. 1). When applicable, specific incentive-based contracts should be awarded. Award-and incentive-fee-type contracts ensure that contractors are rewarded for good performance and high quality assurance. Though the FAR has long required "responsible contractor" determination, the PBC gives the process new emphasis.

PBC also suggests that when acquiring services that have been previously obtained, the agency should rely on past experience and previous data gained from prior contracts. It stresses that when appropriate, conversion from cost-plus fixed-fee to firm fixed-price arrangements should be considered, and it also recommends a shift from level of effort (term) to completion.

PROCUREMENT REFORM INITIATIVE AT USAID

Criticized by the General Accounting Office (GAO 1992a) for a lack of clearly articulated strategic direction and in response to GAO's recommendations, USAID began to develop a management improvement plan in 1993. In June of that year, a GAO report stressed that USAID needed to overhaul its management and personnel system because it was "complex, costly, and unsuited to accomplishing the agency's mission" (GAO1993). Faced with diminished resources and a changed geopolitical reality in a post-Cold War era to meet its obligations, the agency needed to reassess its management and contracting policies, to redefine its mission, and to streamline its organization and staff (GAO 1992b, 1996a).

The agency itself admits in a public document that "when the Clinton Administration came into office in 1994, USAID was a troubled organization. Some observers were calling for the agency's abolition, and there was near-universal agreement that serious management reforms were needed" (USAID 1997a, 33).

In April 1993, Brian Atwood was confirmed as the new USAID administrator. Atwood committed the agency's support to a reform effort and laid out a general framework for restructuring the foreign assistance program. In October of that year, USAID was designated by the NPR as a "reinvention laboratory." This committed USAID to fundamental reform and to demonstrate that it could achieve measurable results.

Based on the recommendations of the NPR, USAID began to focus on fewer and more attainable objectives, streamline its organization and staff, and reform its procurement process. Because of budgetary pressures and its own restructuring, the agency also reduced the number of programs, projects, and field missions operating in different countries. In its report, the NPR developed seven major recommendations and thirty seven proposed actions (NPR 1993a).

The procurement reform at USAID was considered one of the cornerstones of the reform effort within the agency. Along these lines, the Federal Acquisition Regulation was revised as part of the reform initiative and as an effort to restore credibility in the procurement system. In August 1994, Atwood committed the agency's support to a governmentwide pilot project to implement performance-based contracting. Procurement reform had become a centerpiece in a "reengineered" USAID as a way of administering public resources more responsibly and effectively. As he put it, "PBC is an approach which, by focusing on performance, can improve the value the public receives from the services the government provides. The work to be performed is defined in objective, mission-related output terms which emphasize what needs to be done rather than how to do it. This approach provides the means to ensure that the desired performance quality level is achieved, and that payment is made only for services which meet contract standards" (USAID 1994).

As part of the process in a "reengineered" USAID, the agency laid out core values in the design and implementation of its intended reforms. These are: (a) customer focus, (b) managing for results, (c) teamwork, and (d) empowerment and accountability. The "customer" is any individual or organization that receives services or products from USAID or benefits from its programs. The ultimate customers are the recipients of aid; the intermediary providers are the contractors who offer their services to USAID for work they normally do abroad. Managing for results refers to producing measurable results rather than satisfying regulatory or administrative requirements. Teamwork means that customers, procurement staff, and contractors are involved in negotiation, management, and evaluation of activities. But teamwork depends on each player knowing his or her part, role, and responsibility. Empowerment/accountability refers to missions/offices that are now empowered to select and run their own project/programs with less need to defer to Washington. They will be held accountable to achieve results (see FAR 1.102). But how, in practice, they will be held accountable is not specified.

Of the core values mentioned, *managing for results* stands out. USAID is suggesting that this approach is a way of keeping Congress and the American taxpayer informed, because it is a means for tracking performance over time and for judging the success of USAID programs. Based on interviews conducted by the author, some contractors are skeptical of this procedure because the failure of a program might not rest solely on the contractor. On the other hand, others have expressed that they are "behind USAID's efforts to adopt organizational and management tools that will help missions to achieve the objectives set forth in their results frameworks" (Fanning 1996, 4).

From the point of view of procurement, performance-based contracting boils down to writing contracts describing results and not spelling out how the contractor is to do the work. At USAID, that means moving away from level-of-effort contracts and changing the focus of statements of work (SOW) with more specific measurable results that contractors ought to achieve. Most contracts at USAID to date have been written as cost-plus fixed-fee, level-of-effort contracts. In part this is because the nature of development work often lends itself to level-of-effort contracts— results are not easily expressed in objective terms. That is, there is a vague, general idea of results that are hoped to be achieved, but it is not known how. The agency, then, was essentially buying the time of development "experts" to work on the tasks described in the SOW. In this sense, the agency was buying input. As a result, USAID had no way to require the contractors to produce results, because it was more interested in telling contractors how to organize and manage their work. Hence, USAID was responsible for failed performance even if the contractor delivered what had been demanded. This practice of just using the level of effort was common, because there was an implicit assumption that it gave the agency control of the process and, secondly, it avoided the legal hassles that could emerge by try-ing to force a contractor to produce results. A contracting officer admitted that "by requiring little of our contractors we have trained them to expect to deliver little and to organize in ways that actually preclude some of them from accepting responsibility for producing results" (Taber 1996)

Performance-based contracting is one expression of an evolv-ing management philosophy that has yet to fully blossom. However, PBC is only a tool which, if it is to become workable, will help the agency achieve the objectives it has outlined in delivering its pro-grams. For PBC to work, all players must deliver: the missions, the host governments, and the contractors. In the development world there are many intangibles, and the level of control and influence for getting results is always shifting. When projects or programs fail, contractors very seldom assume responsibility for their failure. Contractors are only required to provide certain tasks and not to accomplish the program results.

In accordance with the recommendations of the NPR, USAID now must regularly collect, review, and use information on contrac-tor as well as the agency's performance. For this it has had to adopt a monitoring and evaluation system. All operating units managing program funds are required to monitor and report annually on performance, but the new system is likely only to produce more paperwork. Evaluations are not required but are conducted when needed to answer specific management questions about perfor-mance.

Since 1993, the Office of Procurement at USAID has been dis-cussing how to strengthen contract administration and enforce-ment of contract provisions by overhauling the system. While undergoing management restructuring, the agency has had to become more responsive and learn to work with less. In an effort to transform its image to restore public trust and confidence in its programs, the agency has embarked on post closings and downsiz-ing of personnel. Calling itself a "reinvented" agency, USAID is a "learning organization" embarked on reforming itself. The use of performance information and the changing organizational structure would improve performance outcome. Its ultimate success, however, will be measured by whether this work contributes to the development process of the aid recipients. Another critical issue is improving accountability. Since USAID does not deliver services directly, but rather sets the standards and provides the funding to contractors that do, accounting for service delivery based on past performance is important. Contractor abuse, which has been reported in the media, will not disappear, but USAID has began to consider protection against malfeasant contractors by enforcing suspension and debarments.[1]

A 1996 GAO report stressed that as part of the agency's reform efforts under NPR, "USAID has taken a number of steps to encourage wider participation and increase transparency in USAID procurement" (GAO 1996a, 19). In addition, it has reduced contract-award time by 42 percent, has instituted "better procurement planning" and increased the number of procurement professionals.

Until the middle of the 1990s, USAID did not have a comprehensive system in place to evaluate contractors' performance. In the middle of 1995, as required by FAR 42.1502, the agency put in place a system to evaluate contractors' performance. At the same time, FAR 15.608 required past performance as an evaluation criterion to be used in source selection of all competitive awards.

Although procurement reform at USAID is under way, it has yet to address a comprehensive list of issues raised both internally and externally. Currently, the agency is undertaking a reassessment of burdensome regulations and outmoded procurement management systems. "In the past, there had been a lack of consistency in contracting/grant formats, terms, conditions, and interpretations. Onerous ad hoc technical and financial reports were often imposed on contractors and recipients" (Atlantic Management Center 1997, 2-18). To carry out the government's mandate for a more efficient government that costs less, both performance measurement and evaluation are required to ensure that the agency's resources are deployed efficiently. Performance measures track results and determine whether changes in ongoing activities are required. Evaluations can answer questions on whether results are being achieved.

In 1996, "USAID began using a results framework (Results Review and Results Request or R-4), which includes mission's strategic objectives, intermediate results, and operational indicators to measure missions' progress. The R-4 is intended to link resource allocations and performance. USAID offices said that the R-4 process will be fully incorporated in the fiscal year 1998 budget process" (GAO 1996a, 11).

USAID efforts to adopt organizational and new management tools are commendable. It is part of a reengineering effort to focus on the *what*, not the *how*. However, PBC can also run into short-term difficulties. Some of those problems are inherent in the conversion to PBC. One of these changes is switching from the use of cost-plus firm fixed-fee level of effort to fixed-price and incentive type contracts. The transition requires training and learning the new procedures. Initially, this is bound to result in mistakes.

Since the new system is not yet fully in place, most of the ongoing contracts are still not performance based. Part of the reason is a degree of resistance or simply that the old system is hard for some to abandon. Contracting officers are still reluctant to take the time to conduct evaluations because it would mean a heavier workload that they say current staffing would not be able to handle adequately. Contract administration of PBC involves more paper work than level of effort for both program and procurement staff. Assessing contractor performance will require more man-hours in monitoring and evaluating. Information regarding performance has to be provided first from the contracting officer technical representative (COTR) and from the end users, and only then is the initial assessment forwarded to the contractor for review. After the contractor has had the opportunity to comment, the final assessment is made.

One issue that remains murky is that USAID is encouraging "teamwork," that is, the contractor is now part of the team and operates as a "true partner." This means that the contractor actively participates in the evaluation of his or her performance. Although contractors are now involved in the design and implementation of results, they have a very different agenda, because their objective is to maximize profit. Contractors are motivated mainly by monetary incentives, and it is hard to assume that they will always be responsive to the ambitious strategic objectives that the agency has set for itself, which might not always be achievable. Furthermore, there is fear of engaging in disputes with contractors if the agency denies fees or profits to contractors that do not deliver results or fail to perform adequately. Since this is a relatively new process, program officers do not see much value in PBC because the failure of a program is not always exclusively the fault of the contractor. Finally, mistakes might arise in the process that might cause some USAID staff and contractors to blame the PBC concept.

PAST PERFORMANCE AS A CONTRACT ADMINISTRATION TOOL

FAR subpart 42.15 requires evaluations of a contractor's performance in order to have relevant information and records of contracting firms for use in future source selection. FAR 9.104.3b (January 1997) requires a *satisfactory* performance record from the contractor, and the Federal Acquisition Streamlining Act P.L. 103-355, signed by the president in 1994, states that past performance should be used as an indicator in awarding a contract. Past performance is relevant to determine if the contractor bidding for a contract should receive the award or any future work. Low cost does not always guarantee best value for the government. Thus, past performance reports will be a way for the government to determine if the contractor has provided a measurable acceptable or unacceptable performance.

According to Laurent (1997, 35) "gathering past performance information means being able to rate how the contractors do on the job." Commercial firms normally rely on the information about a contractor's past performance. A past performance record is one of the key differences between government agencies and firms in the private sector, where it plays a crucial role in contract awards.[2] One of the priorities to reform federal procurement practices has been to make them resemble the role they play in the commercial practices of the private sector. Past performance is also viewed as a way of reducing the amount of technical evaluation requirements that are included in the solicitation.

The past performance pledge initiative began in January 1994, but the implementation of past performance actually began with contracts that were to be awarded in fiscal year 1995. The first phase (July 1995 through FY1996) policies and procedures were in place (guidelines, a two-page form, and a rating matrix). But having identified 242 contracts to be completed during this time, only 16 percent were completed. The second phase (FY1997) identified five hundred contracts to evaluate, but the goal was met by only 50 percent. The lessons learned have been that: (1) implementing regulations is much more difficult than promulgating them; (2) simplifying the process as if it were a report card is easier; and (3) making the evaluation process part of contract administration is crucial.

Although a past performance report is not a perfect predictor, it is a useful means to select contractors. Past performance is a scored evaluation that is used to help determine the selection of a contractor for a particular project. USAID's past practices (and still much of its current practice) have allowed contractors to write detail proposals to "win" contracts, even if they do not perform accordingly. There are, however, many smaller contractors who do not often win contracts but have a significantly better performance.

Approximately half of all government procurement expenditures are for services. But the objective measures of performance for service contracts are more difficult to establish. It is especially difficult to specify service quality, output, or results. When an agency evaluates a contractor's past performance, it is seeking information on the firm's work experience and making qualitative judgments about how it has performed. According to Edwards (1995, 26-27), "the evaluation of past performance has to include both objective determinations and subjective assessments." This is particularly important for service contracts, which have been widely criticized for being plagued by cost overruns, delays, and other problems. Using past performance is invoked as a means of overcoming these problems and assuring value for money. The approach, according to Kelman (1994), can live up to its promises if it is properly employed.

The evaluation of past performance includes both objective determinations and subjective assessments. To evaluate past performance, the agency must obtain information or "facts" available to it. That is, it must base that on observations of what the firm did and how the work was done, the relevance of the work performed, and the quality of the work performed. Using past performance information could prove useful to judge the overall quality of the contractor, determines best value in the decision-making process, and serves as an indicator for future performance. In essence, the

agency uses past performance information to judge the overall quality of the firm's performance (Edwards 1995).

To measure performance, contractors are being evaluated on
five performance elements: quality of work, timely performance,
cost performance, customer satisfaction, and end-user satisfaction.
Each element is assigned a rating from 1 to 5, 1 being poor performance and 5 being excellent. In the next chapter, data compiled on
one hundred and sixteen contracts obtained from the Division of
Procurement at USAID is presented and analyzed.

Consistent performance evaluation at USAID has been notably
absent during and after the contract had been closed or the project
ended. In fact, the agency has never systematically used information
on the suppliers to evaluate their performance. Part of the reason
is that "procurement personnel are disinclined to take time to conduct evaluations because of the work involved" (Beausoleil 1997,
39). They see this as an added burden to an already heavy workload.
Judgments about how the contractor did in the past did not prevent
the agency from allowing these contractors to bid for other contracts and thus did not reduce their likelihood of being awarded
another contract. In the past the agency settled mainly for CPFF-
term contracts, which obligate the contractor to devote a specified
level of effort—that is, the minimum required to get the job done.
Now, for contracts worth more than $1 million, there is a past per-
formance criterion in awarding new contracts.

Adding past performance in contracts as a factor in evaluation
has its advantages in improving a contractor's performance and
could promise best value. Moreover, the effort to use past performance reports not only can make proposal preparation easier but
would make proposal evaluation more objective. If the contractor
has a track record of performing poorly, then the government must
determine if the contractor is worthy of another contract.
Accountability then becomes an important factor in setting the
standards if excellence in performance is being sought. The criteria
for past performance are established at the beginning of the process
and the contractor is aware of it. An established firm that has successfully satisfied its customers should be recognized for that,
whereas others with poor past performance will have to mend their
ways.

Information about a contractor's performance, although concise, must be inclusive and simple. In the case of USAID it is the contracting officer technical representative (COTR) who provides some of the essential information that goes in the Contractor Performance Report. The performance evaluations bring together the COTR and the contracting officer (CO), who divide their responsibilities to fill out the report by reviewing and making the initial assessment. The evaluation is based on documented records (e.g., financial reports on cost control). All multiyear contracts at USAID must now have annual interim reports and then a final evaluation at the completion of activities and closing out the contract. The form provides space to comment on five specific areas to measure satisfaction with the contractor's performance. Each comment must be accompanied by a numeral rating on five aspects of performance. COs can be very precise or they can provide additional commentary. The report also provides space for comments on key personnel utilized for contract implementation. In concluding the report, the CO makes an overall assessment and assigns a mean score on the overall performance of the contractor (USAID 1997b).

After reviewing and making the assessment, the performance report is sent to the contractor for review. The contractor may contest the evaluation and has thirty days to respond. If the contractor disagrees with the ratings or scores, he or she must make it known in writing to the CO. If the CO and the contractor cannot come to an agreement, the final decision is made by a higher level official at the agency. An agreement may finally be reached, and the final score stays as such for the record.

The danger with allowing the contractor to challenge low ratings by USAID is that the agency may not be willing to give bad ratings for fear of long, drawn-out disputes. The challenge of low ratings and the subsequent rebuttal and negotiation of it is also likely to result in inflating the scores on the contractor's performance.

The evidence gathered for this study shows that of 116 contracts, approximately one-fifth were challenged by contractors. In some cases the score given was increased to a higher and more agreeable overall score by both parties. Since 3 is an average score that meets the requirements, most of the disputed ratings came when the score was below 3.

Although the concept of past performance has been praised, there are also criticisms at the way past performance is used. Some would argue that it represents a barrier to entry for small and less advantaged firms in winning contracts if it results in setting up long-term relationships with a few suppliers. As Burman (1997) puts it, "some see it just as another tool to use arbitrarily in selecting business partners: the least favored need not apply."

Past performance reports are nothing new. The method is only new in some specific details and it is a simplified version of techniques used for decision analysis. The appeal of past performance is that certain benefits could be derived, making it an effective tool of contract management. The most difficult problem confronting the government is finding reliable information to make assessments on the quality of performance of the contractors. Furthermore, the government often has to be on the defensive when there is disagreement with the scores, which weakens the process. And finally, there is still some resistance on the part of contracting officers to use it because of the added administrative burden.

NOTES

1. The list of abuse and misuse of aid is long, but for our purposes we can mention just a few. Some of the most recent incidents are documented in Robbins and Leisman 1997; Eaton 1996; Myers 1997; and USAID whistle-blower, Paul Neifer before the Committee on International Relations of the U.S. Congress, in 1997. Within USAID there have also been many instances of corruption that have been well documented in *The Washington Post*. Other instances of suspicion of fraud and abuse by whistle-blowers have often been ignored or silenced by the agency. See Linda D. Whitclock, "Speaking Out: One USAID Whistle Blower's Sour Note," *Foreign Service Journal* 74, No. 4 April 1997. As far as this author is concerned, none of the twenty five largest contractors has ever been challenged or sanctioned by USAID for wrongdoing.

2. There is little hard data comparing government and private contracts. What is known is that the government wants to adopt a more businesslike attitude in the contracting process by using past performance information as a way of selecting contractors.

7

Empirical Evidence on USAID Contracts

This chapter explores how USAID's contracting process is consistent with the criteria for optimal practices, as specified by the McAfee and McMillan (1988) model. The McAfee and McMillan model of contracting serves as a benchmark against which the contracting process at USAID can be compared, and it is used here to determine if the agency is awarding the optimal contract. The model includes types of contracts and the circumstances under which a contract would be optimal. To test the rationale of the model, regression analysis is used to determine whether the agency is getting best value and whether the procurement process is generating desirable outcomes.

A model is by its very nature a simplification of reality. Nevertheless, there may be lessons to be drawn from such a model because it simulates aspects of the real economy. Contracting theory provides some insights into the relationship between what is optimal from the point of view of the government, besides providing a basis for analyzing the widespread use of contracting for disbursement of foreign development assistance. The approach adopted here also helps us understand the motivation of firms in opting for government contracts most advantageous to them and shows that the government can reduce its payments to firms if it uses the optimal contract.

THE DATA, SAMPLE, AND EXPLANATORY VARIABLES

The research questions addressed in this study are as follows: Is the contracting process competitive? Are the contracts that are awarded judged to lead to desirable outcomes based on the criteria established by USAID? Is the government getting the best value for the contracts it awards? The research questions are aimed at gathering information that will provide a clear, comprehensive picture of current USAID contracting practices. Much of the information used for this analysis is drawn from data gathered from the agency's closed out contracts, from the agency's past performance evaluation data bank, and from interviews with government officials.

The main source of data comes from USAID's Office of Procurement. A sample of 116 closed-out contracts were analyzed to examine the role of contracts in the delivery of foreign assistance. The data compiled is for a ten-year period, from 1988 through 1997 (see appendix A). The 116 contracts were chosen at random. Each contract file and past performance report contained much important data such as project purpose and objective, amount of contract awarded, contract type, duration of contract, location of project, home base of contractor, and other data. This has enabled us to examine contractor behavior, to ascertain whether these contracts are cost-effective and optimal, and to measure the performance outcome of each contract.

The closed-out contracts were divided into the three categories discussed previously: *fixed-price, cost-plus,* and *incentive.* Of these 116 contracts, thirty three were fixed-price, seventy eight were cost-plus, and five were incentive-type contracts. To analyze the effect of the policy, the total number of contracts was evenly divided into two periods (1988-1993 and 1994-1997) after the policy of "reinventing government" was instituted.

The analysis presented here provides a basis for comparison of types of contracts and ways to measure performance. The rest of the data, compiled from official government sources, provides contextual information that sheds light on market structure, contracting practices, and contract payments. Other sources of references for the study are two sets of interviews conducted by the author with both the CEOs of private contracting firms and senior USAID procurement officials to take into account their views of the contracting process at the agency. Conclusions are drawn by analyzing the implications involved in the use of one type of contract over others that tend to result in relative savings and generate greater efficiency.

Contracting theory tells us that there are essentially three different kinds of procurement contracts: the fixed-price contract, the cost-plus contract, and the incentive contract. The theory tells us that the preferred types of contracts—from the point of view of the government—are fixed-price and incentive contracts (McCall 1970; Moore 1967; McAfee and McMillan 1988). The former is particularly appropriate for the procurement of specific goods. The latter is generally considered most appropriate for the procurement of services. In a fixed-price contract, the government payment is simply the firm's bid. In an incentive-type contract, the payment depends both on the bid and on realized costs. Some incentive contracts provide that if the costs come in below estimates, the government and contractor share the savings. If realized costs exceed the firm's bid, the contractor is responsible for part of the cost overrun. However, in a cost-plus type of contract (e.g., cost-plus fixed-fee), the government agrees to cover all the costs incurred by the contractor, plus pay a fee that is fixed in advance or is a proportion of costs.

When USAID wants to contract for a development project in an LDC, it usually calls for bids from interested firms, and the bidder that has the best technical proposal and shows reasonable costs is selected. The winning bidder, however, is not always the lowest-cost bidder. Before calling for bids, the government agency also specifies the type of contract (fixed-price, cost reimbursement, or incentive-type contract) and it applies its selection criteria to determine its preferred contractor. Thus the agency lays out the framework and sets the procedure for determining the service or project in the solicitation. In specifying the type of contract, it tries to choose among bidders who will minimize costs. After awarding the contract, the agency must then audit and maintain records of contract costs and performance.

BASIC ASSUMPTIONS

The model used by McAfee and McMillan is a theoretical conceptual construction that relates us to understand the types of contracts awarded, the behavior of firms competing for such contracts, and the motivations of the government to award the contracts. The model shows that the government could reduce its expenditures to firms if it chooses the optimal contract. The three types of contracts can be depicted graphically as shown in Figure 7.1. P and C denote price and cost. P is the bidding price and what the government pays. The fixed-price contract is the horizontal line where the price is set at Po. The cost-plus contract is depicted as a diagonally drawn line from the origin. As the contracts vary from 0 to 1, the move is from fixed-cost to cost-plus.

From the government's point of view, a fixed-price contract involves the least risk and is preferable because the firm bears all the risk. It is also preferable when the project attracts a sufficient number of bidders to ensure that competition will hold down the fee the government will pay.

The pure cost-plus contract is never optimal if there is more than one potential contractor. For risky projects, the government may not be able to attract qualified bidders without agreeing to take on risk itself. In the cost-plus contract, the government takes on all the project's risk. It is thus not an optimal contract in terms of cost and should be used only when circumstances necessitate it.

Figure 7.1
Types of Contracts

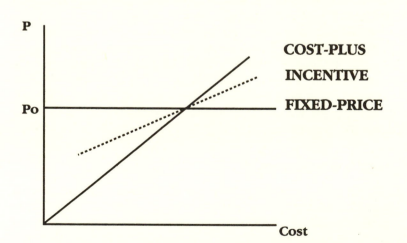

The McAfee and McMillan model can also be depicted graphically in Figure 7.2. Here it is assumed that the government chooses the level of cost-share parameter α. The optimal design of a government contract is in determining the value of α^* that will, on average, minimize the government's payments. By changing, it can increase or reduce its expected payments to firms. MB denotes marginal benefit (the rate at which government payments decline); α increases with MB. MC denotes the marginal cost (the rate at which the government's expected payments rise as α rises). As α increases, expected government payments decrease because of the risk-sharing effect of the risk-averse firm's bid. On the other hand, as α increases, the government may pay more. The optimal value is α^*, where MC = MB. Thus if the value α^* at which the marginal cost curve and the marginal benefit curve intersect is less than 0, then the optimal value of α is zero, and the fixed-price contract is a more efficient contract for the government. When α^* lies between 0 and 1, the best contract is an incentive contract.

Figure 7.2
Government Optimization

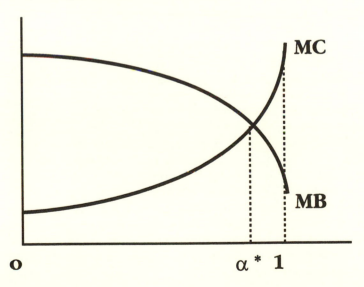

To sum up, the McAfee and McMillan model stresses that only under certain circumstances is a contract very close to a cost-plus optimal. Such a contract would be an incentive contract with a cost-share parameter α close to 1, so that almost all of any cost over-run would be borne by the government. In the incentive contract, the risk is shared. Contractors who fail share in the penalty, rather than the government alone. Contractors who succeed reap extra profits, and are rewarded for their risk taking and their efficient operation. For incentive contracts (0< α < 1), the larger the α is, the lower the government's expected payment.

METHOD OF ANALYSIS

A linear regression model was applied as the appropriate technique for investigating optimal contract related questions. The dependent variable is contractor performance outcome.[1] The independent variables used are: contract type, cost, timeliness, quality, and contract value.

The ordinary least squares (OLS) regression model explaining performance outcome from the point of view of USAID and the LDC (end-users or beneficiaries) are as follows:

YUSAID = a + bxcontract type - cxcontract value + dxcost control + exquality + fxtimeliness + error

YLDC = a + bxcontract type - cxcontract value + dxcost control + exquality + fxtimeliness + error

Contract type is dichotomous and contract value is a continuous independent variable that do not have a numerical rating but have an association to the other independent variables (cost, quality, timeliness) that are measured by a single number on a scale of 1 to 5.

In order to obtain firsthand information about contracting and try to learn to what degree policy changes have affected the procurement process, two questionnaires were formulated, one for USAID procurement officials, and one for private contractors. Fifteen USAID contracting officers and ten representatives from private contractors responded to the questionnaires. Open-ended interviews were conducted with the twenty five respondents to gather more in-depth information about the procurement process at USAID.

Analysis of Data

The most commonly used type of contract by USAID is *cost-plus*. The reasons provided by agency contracting officers are that costs cannot easily be determined because of the nature of development work, which carries many intangibles. This uncertainty makes it difficult to agree on a price. *Cost-reimbursement* (or *cost-plus*) types of contracts are divided into term and completion. Under cost-plus fixed-fee (CPFF)-*term,* the contract obligates the contractor to devote only a specified level of effort. The CPFF-*completion* specifies the end product, which the contractor is required to complete and deliver. However, if the contractor just simply finishes the work, it is not always an optimal contract because the agency is not getting best value. *Incentive* type contracts, on the other hand, are designed to motivate the contractor with incentives that will, it is hoped, result in providing better quality, speed, and reliability at a reasonable cost.

USAID contracting differs in many respects from more conventional economic activities, and in some ways from other government agencies. One major difference is the use of mainly *cost-plus fixed-fee* contracts, which account for nearly three-fourths of procurement outlays at the agency. Prices are not always set on a competitive basis but are often fixed by negotiation on an estimate of actual cost. Under CPFF the government agrees to reimburse within limits all allowable costs incurred by the contractor. For this reason the CPFF contract provides weaker or no incentives for cost reductions and efficiency (Scherer 1964). *Incentive* contracts such as *award-fee* are not as commonly used, but under the "reinvention" effort to restructure procurement, the agency has tried to encourage the use of these types of contracts because they promise a better performance outcome (USAID 1997a).

The data that form the empirical basis of this study suggest that the agency is in fact using mainly *cost-plus* types of contracts, which, from the point of view of the government, are not usually optimal, and that *fixed-price* and *incentive* types of contracts, which could carry lower contract payments, are not as commonly used. Based on the data compiled, approximately 67 percent of the contracts are *cost-reimbursement,* and the rest are *fixed-price* and *incentive* type of contracts. However, based on discussions held with procurement officials, the author was informed that USAID has been using *cost-reimbursement* contracts (mainly CPFF) in more than 80 percent of its contracts awarded.

Table 7.1 shows the distribution of contract types before and after the Government Performance and Results Act of 1993 and the NPR policy of "reinventing government" was put in place. Although the sample size is too small to make any definitive statement on types of contracts awarded by USAID, it indicates that the majority of the contracts awarded are still cost-plus fixed-fee. Although there is a decrease in number and percentage of cost-plus after the policy changed, it should be noted that the pre-policy (1993) covers a six-year period (1988-1993), and the post-1993 period covers only four years (1994-1997). The number of incentive contracts remains about the same for both periods, but there is a marked increase in the use of fixed-price contracts.[2]

Although one can only generalize from the cases considered in this study, they still provide a good source and a starting point to determine if USAID is using the most effective and cost-efficient contracts. The results of this research should also tell us whether USAID, in the context of "reinventing government," is achieving high marks in terms of performance outcome in the contracts awarded.

The data in the appendix show all the types of contracts awarded by USAID. All these variations have been collapsed into three different categories (FP, CP, and IC) that are appropriate for this study. There are also five variables associated with each contract (quality, cost control, timeliness, USAID satisfaction, and LDC or end-user satisfaction). Conceptually, we want to explain to what extent these variables determine the degree of performance outcome for both USAID (the customer) and the end-users (LDCs).

Table 7.2 summarizes contractor performance as an overall assessment at the end of these contracts by type of contract. The scores are provided on a five point scale from *poor* (1) to *outstanding* (5). The table shows that it is the middle value average that predominates. Hence, one can infer from these data that contractor performance is not a convincing "success" if the mean score, in terms of its equivalent, as if it were a report card, is only "average" or C grade (*good*) for most of the contracts. As a form of quality control that would positively affect contractor performance, the system is being praised by agency officials, but in terms of actual

Table 7.1
Distribution of USAID Contracts

	FIXED-PRICE				COST-PLUS				INCENTIVE				TOTAL		
	1988-1993		1994-1997		1988-1993		1994-1997		1988-1993		1994-1997		1988-1993		1994-1997
	number	%*	number	%	number	%	number	%	number	%	number	%	number	%**	number	%
	5	4.3%	28	24.1%	51	44%	27	23.3%	2	1.7%	3	2.6%	58	50%	58	50%
Percentage of total	28.4%				67.2%				4.3%				100%			

*This is based on the marginal total.
**This is based on the total number of contracts.
*Source:*Appendix.

Table 7.2
USAID Contracts Summary Statistics, N=116

PERFOMANCE OUTCOME CRITERIA	FIXED PRICE* N = 33			COST PLUS N = 78			INCENTIVE N = 5		
	Mean Score	Stand. Div.	Min/Max	Mean Score	Stand Div	Min/Max	Mean Score	Stand Div	Min/Max
QUALITY	3.652	.643	3.0/5.0	3.229	.846	1.0/5.0	3.800	.837	3.0/5.0
COST	3.250	.458	2.5/4.0	3.229	.837	1.0/5.0	3.800	1.30	2.0/5.0
ON-TIME	3.333	.854	2.0/5.0	3.004	.697	1.0/5.0	3.400	1.14	2.0/4.0
USAID SATISFACTION	3.712	.673	3.0/5.0	3.385	.702	2.0/5.0	4.200	.447	4.0/5.0
LDC SATISFACTION	3.500	.635	2.5/5.0	3.356	.704	2.0/5.0	3.800	.447	3.0/4.0
Average Performance	3.489	.472	2.6/4.6	3.282	.572	1.8/4.8	3.800	.678	3.0/4.6

* Under fixed price (1) there are only 8 contracts. Other types of contracts: time and materials (5) there are 2 and under ID/IQ or indefinite quantity contract (6) there are 4. Both of these contracts are similar to fixed-price, which is why they have been collapsed under (1).

Source: USAID, Office of Procurement

results, better performance (*very good* = 4) appears less frequently and *excellent* (5) is altogether absent and is yet to be achieved.

Table 7.3 also shows that if the performance scores for the three types of contracts are compared, it is incentive contracts (IC) that score higher, whereas fixed-price (FP) is better than cost-plus fixed fee (CPFF). The differences in mean score, however, indicate that with the exception of USAID satisfaction, there is no statistically significant difference among the three types of contracts. The analysis of variance results showed that the means are statistically different. In conducting a multiple comparison of the three means using the Scheffe test, the results showed that *fixed-price* has a statistically significant higher mean score than *cost-plus*, whereas there is no statistical difference between *incentive* type and *cost-plus*.

Performance is defined and measured with respect to the needs and concerns of the client (in this case USAID) and the end-users or less developed countries served. Effectiveness and efficiency are two important dimensions of performance, also referred to as performance indicators. Effectiveness has been defined with respect to achieving the goals and objectives of a service (Epstein 1992). Effectiveness also refers to the ratio comparing the quality of the service provided with the cost. Performance measurement is important to improve decision making, to improve accountability, and to improve the service being delivered.

Effectiveness thus encompasses both quality and quantity aspects of service. For example, public transit effectiveness depends not only on the number of people who use it, but also whether it is safe, timely, and reliable. Efficiency may be more difficult to measure precisely than effectiveness. To measure effectiveness one might have to consider cost accounting, controlling for acceptable quality of work, and the level of difficulty of the work. These measures of performance can help USAID officials provide assistance that is more responsive to the needs and desires of the end-users. Thus they can also improve operations and responsiveness to changes in development work.

Table 7.3 does not show a significant relationship among the three different types of contracts. A reason may be that there are only five cases of *incentive-* type contracts and thirty three types of *fixed-price*. To better understand the association between the contracts in this small sample, I have collapsed FP and IC to measure

Table 7.3
Contractor Performance in Meeting USAID and LDC Expectations

VARIABLES	COEFFICIENT (Performance/USAID)	STANDARD ERROR	COEFFICIENT (Performance/LDC)	STANDARD ERROR
Intercept (constant)	1.39 (t=4.06, p<.000)	.34	1.76(t=4.55, p<.001)	.387
Type of Contract*	-.223 (t = -2.11, p=.037)	.10	-.04 (t=.366, p=.715)	.120
Contract Value	-.000006 (t = -1.94, p= 0.54)	.00	-.000008 (t=-.215, p=.252)	.000
Cost Control	.257 (t= 3.82, p<.001)	.06	.08 (t=1.15, p.252)	.076
Quality	.407 (t=4.91, p<.001)	.08	.470 (t=4.99, p<.001)	.094
On Time	.09 (t= 1.09, p<.277)	.08	-.04 (t=-.425, p<.672)	.097
R^2	.50 (F=21.51, p<.001) Adjusted R^2 = .47	.51	.31 (F=9.83, p<.001) Adjusted R^2 = .28	.57

* Type of contract refers to the following: (1) is both fixed-price and incentive type contract, (0) is cost-plus.
*Source:*Table 4 and Appendix.

them against CPFF. The results are provided in Table 7.4 where the left-hand side (performance/USAID) shows that the t ratios are highly significant. The variable type of contract shows a strong association for performance outcome as measured by the rating system used by the agency that meets USAID expectations (t = -2.11, p =.037). The same is true for cost control (t = 3.82, p < .001) and quality (t = 4.91, p < .001). However, the right side of the table, which depicts contractor performance as assessed by LDC "satisfaction," presents a somewhat different picture. In the case of LDCs, the type of contract is not important (p = .715) and neither is cost control (p = .252) and contract value (p = .033), but quality is significant (p < .001).

The OLS regression explains contractor performance outcome based on the evaluation ratings given by USAID. It measures whether contractor performance has fulfilled the expectations of USAID as well as those of the LDCs. Y*USAID* represents performance/USAID and Y*LDC* represents performance/LDC regression equations. The adjusted R^2 shows that 47 percent of the variation in USAID satisfaction is explained collectively by the five independent variables. But information on performance as assessed by LDC "satisfaction" has to be taken with caution, because the R^2 in this case explains only 28 percent of the change. The reason behind this outcome is that there may be other variables that are not considered in the equation that could explain more fully LDC "satisfaction" with contractor performance. The results should not be surprising, given the different expectations of LDCs and their heterogeneity, which would require the use of other variables.

The evidence is consistent with the theory that incentive contracts and fixed-price contracts are better or preferable to CPFF-term. These results, therefore, confirm the initial assertion that optimal incentive contracts and fixed-price contracts minimize payments for the government. Since we are mainly interested in contractor performance/USAID, the information on the independent variables does a better job in explaining performance/USAID than "satisfaction" as assessed from the LDCs' point of view. Consistent with the theory, the factors that increase government cost overruns and lead to only average performance make the use of incentive type contracts more feasible.

Table 7.4 compares contractor performance USAID and LDC

Table 7.4
Contract Types in Measuring Contractor Performance

Variables	Coefficient Performance/ USAID	Standard Error	t value (p value)	Coefficient Performance/ LDC	Standard Error	t value (p value)
Intercept	.97	.26	3.68 (p < .001)	1.69	.29	5.68 (p < .001)
Type of Contract* cost plus = 0 incentive = 1 fixed price = 0	.41	.24	2.04 (p < .043)	.24	.27	.892 (p < =.374)
Type of Contract cost plus = 0 incentive = 0 fixed price = 1	.18	.11	1.63 (p = .105)	.01	.12	.08 (p = .930)
Contract Value	-.000007	.000	-1.99 (p = .048)	-.000008	.00	-2.19 (p = .030)
Cost Control	.24	.06	3.62 (p < .001)	.07	.07	1.02 (p = 3.08)
Quality	.41	.08	4.91 (p < .001)	.47	.09	4.96 (p < .001)
On Time	.09	.08	1.14 (p = .257)	-.03	.09	-.379 (p = .705)
R^2	R^2 = .50 Adj R^2 = .48	.51	F = 18.27 (p < .001)	R^2 = .32 Adj R^2 = .28	.65	F = 8.28 (p < .001)

*The effects of the type of contract were calculated with respect to the cost-plus which is set at 0.
Source: Table 4 and Appendix.

satisfaction based on contract type performance. Here the two types of contracts (*fixed-price*, *cost-plus*) are compared. Because of the small number of cases for *incentive* contracts, I have collapsed these into the *fixed-price* category. The coefficients for both IC and FP are significant and show that other things being equal, performance/USAID is highest for *incentive* type contracts. The other coefficients (contract value, cost control, timeliness, and quality) are significant and show that performance, or "satisfaction" as the agency calls it, decreases when the value of the contract is high. Similarly, contractor performance increases when cost is kept under control. Finally, performance outcome is reflected in the degree of significance of the quality variable. Performance in the case of ratings reflecting LDC "satisfaction" in fulfilling the requirements show that only quality is significant and, therefore, most important to the recipients of aid.

The adjusted R^2 measures the variability of "satisfaction" with contractor performance. The left-hand side of the variable shows that 48 percent of the variability of contractor performance from USAID's point of view is explained by type of contract, contract value, cost control, and quality, when the contracts are grouped CP, FP, IC. For LDCs, on the right hand side of the table, only 28 percent of variability can be explained. This is because quality is the most significant variable and contract value is also important.

SURVEY RESULTS

To gather information on contracting with USAID, a questionnaire was prepared for the agency's contracting officers. It had questions regarding the bidding process and performance evaluation at USAID. The respondents then met with the author in face-to-face interviews. The purpose was to gather more in-depth information as well as the respondent's explanations of the award process at USAID and of the evaluation process.

The questionnaire/interview process arose both from the specific questions, which reflect practices accepted by economists and by the business world as efficient and economically sound, and from the broader question of whether the "reinvention" the agency undertook is seeing results.

To address these issues, both questionnaire and interview questions focused on procurement. Is it competitive, as it would be in a business environment? Are fixed-price and incentive contracts used, or at least recognized as superior? What are the reasons for continued use of cost-plus contracts? Are evaluations being used to help make better procurement decisions and weed out poor performers? If not, why not?

Seven of the 15 contracting officers who responded to the survey indicated that they agreed with the statement that "USAID's policies and procedures ensure that competitive procurement is fair and open." The remainder said that some factors give bidders an advantage; some indicated that larger firms have an edge in the process, and some said that firms with previous contracts have an advantage.

Although there was no consensus on what would improve the competitive process, some stressed that the use of past performance information would make the process easier and more competitive. Others said that the use of an oral presentation or multiple task order contracting would improve things: "Existing process, if followed, is fine," said one, and another said the process would be improved by "better education of COTRs and project officers regarding the roles and responsibilities of technical evaluation committee members."

Regarding the most common problems encountered with contractors, the responses referred mainly to cost overruns, improper billing, poor understanding of contract requirements, and delays in performance scheduling.

Although more than half responded "Yes" to the question of whether current USAID policies and procedures are adequate to deal with poor performers, a number of them disagreed. Two said that the issue was implementation of existing systems and manpower shortages. Another responded, "Too many COTRs and COs are reluctant to take action to make them perform or terminate."

Interviews with questionnaire in hand were also conducted with for-profit USAID contractors. The questions asked referred to the degree of competition, size of the firm, contract award, and contractor's performance. Those interviewed were generally the CEOs or the contract managers of the firm. The respondents were picked from the twenty five largest firms whose line of work is mainly development.

Ten of those respondents stated that seventy of 100 of their firm's total business, in terms of dollar income, is with USAID. Their total revenue for the last fiscal year ranged from $30 million to $500 million. Most of the firms also revealed that they spend anywhere from $10,000 to $300,000 in putting together a proposal and competing for a contract, depending on the size of the contract award. The average expenditure in competing for a contract runs around $45,000 for many of these firms. The respondents were asked to estimate what percentage of the time they win USAID contracts for which their firms bid. The responses ranged from 25 to 70 percent of the time. Firms that said they win about one out of three bids include Development Alternatives, Chemonics International, and Abt Associates. Those that said they win about one out of two or a higher percentage include PADCO and the Academy for Educational Exchange.

When asked how USAID compares with other government agencies in its contracting process, one respondent said, "USAID has many regulations." Another called USAID's system "more idiosyncratic—it's like no other." The same respondent said that USAID's "modus operandi is changing so contractors have to adapt to new rules. This has created some strain, since both (contractors and the agency) are trying to learn new contracting mechanisms."

Another criticized USAID contracting procedure as "difficult, time-consuming, and financially burdensome. Contracts with USAID are complex. They need to simplify." But another said that USAID is "unique, more challenging, more rewarding, more relationship-based."

Regarding RFPs, one respondent said, "Their RFPs are poorly written and usually don't have enough information." A number of them said RFPs were unclear or sloppily written. Asked about the effects of performance-based contracting, a number of them said it has not made a difference since their performance has been rated well. Others said this has made the whole process more difficult. And one said it had not been implemented well: "We like the approach in theory. Again, USAID is having a hard time actually doing performance-based contracting. They cannot keep their hands off micromanagement."

Most said they felt past performance evaluations will have a positive effect on contractor performance, although one said, "if done correctly, positive. Now they are just irritating." In general, then, several of the largest contractors found USAID's contracting procedure cumbersome and inefficient. A number of them criticized the implementation of evaluation, though not the concept.

SUMMARY FINDINGS

The theoretical model employed in this study indicated that incentive and fixed-price contracts would be most appropriate for a government agency. The model shows that those contracts minimize risk and cost for the government, whereas the third type, cost-plus, tends to shift risk and cost to the government and push up contract costs. Although the results of my analysis are only suggestive, they are very much in line with what the model predicts—that is, that cost-plus contracts have resulted in lower performance outcome as measured by the agency. Several reasons for USAID's failure to switch to the types of contracts more likely to produce better performance are suggested—concern over adjustment cost problem (e.g., monitoring and more extensive evaluations), the influence of the contractors, who benefit from the system as it is, and the difficulty of making sweeping changes in a large, entrenched bureaucracy.

NOTES

1. USAID performance reports use the term *satisfaction* and assign numerical ratings to contractors based on an evaluation of the extent to which contractor performance fulfilled the expectations of USAID as well as those of LDCs. USAID performance rating refers to customer "satisfaction" as reflected in the COTR's and CO's evaluation. It is the business relation between the contractor and the contract administrator (in this case USAID). It rates the standard in meeting expectations on contract objectives. LDC performance rating refers to "satisfaction" of the end-users or beneficiaries of the product or service as measured by the agency. Contractors are rated based on their performance on whether product or service "satisfied" customer needs

2. The data shows only eight FP-type contracts. But as the term *fixed-price* is used here, it also includes other types of contracts that are somewhat similar, such as time and materials and indefinite quantity contracts.

8

More Bang for Your Buck: Old Wine in New Bottles?

HOW MUCH HAS PROCUREMENT CHANGED?

The findings of this study reveal some weaknesses in the system of awarding contracts at USAID. The study also takes note of the changing role of U.S. development assistance and supports greater use of fixed-price and award fee-type contracts. This is consistent with two recent trends. First, the agency is increasingly relying on outsiders (contractors and non-governmental organizations, or NGOs) to carry out development work and second, development is mainly intended to enhance the capacity of the private sector in less developed countries (LDCs). The trends reflect a global shift toward privatization and greater reliance on market forces.

The theoretical and statistical analyses of the previous chapter suggest that the optimal contract, from the point of view of the government, is fixed-price for the purchase of goods and incentive-type for the procurement of services. Choosing these types of contracts over level-of-effort (CPFF-term) can result in lower payments on development assistance by the government, facilitate a more comprehensive monitoring and evaluation of the contracts, and conform more to the performance-based contracting approach that seeks to obtain better performance outcome.

The theoretical model and empirical results of the cases would suggest that incentive contracts (e.g., award-fee) are more appropriate for USAID. This study has given special attention to incentive type contracts because payment is dependent upon contractor performance and evaluation is more clearly focused on results. Cost overruns, as previously mentioned, are less frequent and much smaller in incentive-type contracts than in CPFF contracts. A cost-plus (cost-reimbursement) contract gives the contractor little incentive to keep realized costs low, because any increase in costs is simply passed on to the government.

The fixed-price contract also has the advantage of providing strong incentives for cost control: the contractor bears the full burden of any cost overrun. According to the theoretical model, the fixed-price contract is optimal if the bidders are risk neutral and if there are many bidders.

Although the use of cost-reimbursement contracts has its drawbacks, USAID uses cost-reimbursement contracts most frequently. More than 70 percent of the contracts awarded are CPFF (level-of-effort); the agency uses incentive-type contracts (e.g., award fee) very infrequently. The main argument put forth as to why USAID uses mainly level-of-effort cost-reimbursement type contracts is that because of the nature of development work, level-of-effort is more appropriate. Results are often not easily expressed in objective terms. In most instances, the agency has only just a general idea of the results it hopes to obtain, or how best to achieve them. Thus, agency officials say, the choice of CPFF is justified.

The use of cost-plus-or cost-reimbursement-type contracts generally means lower risks and higher profits for contractors. Once the contractor has been selected, that contractor has a reason to raise rather than reduce costs. The government has encouraged contracting officers to focus on contractor profit rates (profits as a percentage of cost) rather than on the total price of the project or program (cost-plus profit). This practice has a perverse effect: the higher the estimated cost of the project or program, the higher the profit considered appropriate for the contractor. It thus provides a disincentive for a contractor to run a low-cost operation.

Incentive-type contracts, on the other hand, guarantee the contractor an increase in profit for reductions in cost or for high-quality performance. In addition, these contracts are generally better managed because contractors are required to provide timely information on progress and are evaluated against predetermined goals and objectives. The slowness in switching to incentive contracts at USAID is owing in part to contracting officers' unfamiliarity with them. There is also a degree of resistance because such types of contracts would increase the workload in terms of monitoring and evaluating performance.

The contractor's concern is to maximize profit over the length of the contract. The government, on the other hand, tries to persuade the contractor to avoid significant cost overruns. But for the contractor, lowering costs may result in mean lower profits. The feasible solution, then, is to offer contracts higher profits as they reduce costs. This means introducing mechanisms that ensure that cost savings will be shared with contractors, thereby providing financial incentives for cost control.

This study reveals that CPFF-term contracts, as used by USAID, do not provide adequate incentives for cost control; nor do they operate efficiently: hence the agency's "about average" satisfaction with contractors' performance. The results reported in this study reveal that fixed-price and incentive contracts performed better than CPFF-type contracts. Thus, the government would save money if it were using fewer CPFF type contracts.

Desirable contractor performance is efficient and provides the best value. The contractor should accomplish specific results on time and at a reasonable cost. In the simplest conception, the agency argues that performance is based on quality, on whether the contracts are accomplished on time, and whether costs are kept to a minimum. Given this frame of reference, this research shows that in general, contracts awarded by USAID have not been optimal, costs are unnecessarily high, and the concentration of contracts remains in a handful of firms.

In the past relatively little emphasis was placed on satisfactory past performance as a criterion for future selection. USAID now has in place a performance evaluation system designed to collect information on a contractor's performance for use in future source selection. The data presented here indicate that, on the whole, contractor performance has been only slightly better than average. In the context of the agency's efforts to reform itself, this tells us that there is still much improvement to be made. Moreover, past performance will need to address yet another problem: most of the major contractors have a number of projects under way at this time. In some they perform well and in others they perform poorly. How is the firm penalized if it has an established record and conducts regular business with the agency? It is unlikely that the contractor will be denied new contracts because it scored poorly in some. How, then, are the good and the not-so-good job performances blended together to create an index of overall firm performance? Finally, there is the issue of negotiating the scores with contractors when the scores given are below average. Clearly, a system that allows the party being evaluated to upgrade a score is flawed and is unlikely to weed out poor performers.

Observable problems with contractor performance also can be seen from two opposite perspectives. Several of the contractors who responded to the survey said that USAID's RFPs, which contain the statement of work (SOW), are often vaguely specified and do not provide precise information on what is expected. When contractors negotiate the contract, their suggestions on making the project operational are often incorporated. Moreover, upon completion of the contract, overall performance evaluation also can be negotiated if it does not meet the expectations of the contractor. Contractors thus have a great deal of influence on how contracts are set up, and on how they are evaluated as well. Yet contracting officers stress that problems often emanate from a poor understanding of the contract by the contractors. The use of past performance is in many respects a subjective process, and those making the subjective judgments may be influenced by a number of factors that make selection arbitrary. Although the policy specifying what is needed is now performance- based, there is still a lot of misunderstanding of what that is. Performance-based (PBC) contracting means specifying to the extent practicable what you want and setting performance standards. However, the agency has a long way to go in training people with both PBC and past performance.

An examination of USAID's contractors reveals that twenty five firms are awarded the vast majority of the contracts. Procurement preference toward the larger, more established firms leads to a degree of reduction in competition and raises the amount the government pays for development projects. Faced with budget constraints, the agency seems to be awarding fewer contracts but contracts of greater dollar value. Additionally, there are enduring procurement management problems that need to be resolved, such as more adequate training of personnel, if the agency is to award the optimal contracts.

CAN GOVERNMENT BE REINVENTED?

One of the persistent criticisms of USAID has been that the agency has failed to promote large-scale development in most of the countries where it operates. As a result, many observers and official reports have acknowledged that the agency was in need of a major overhaul. For a number of years, some of the problems associated with the lack of impact on development was linked to the fact that USAID's program objectives were too numerous, that the agency lacked focus, had poor management, and was unable to properly assess the impact of its programs.

However, calls to restructure the agency were not new. Under different administrators, recommendations to restructure its functions to achieve its overall objectives have been made since USAID was created to promote socioeconomic development. Although accusations that recipient governments often misuse aid money and mismanage projects might be accurate, USAID is still the one that dictates policies to aid-recipient countries.

Under the "reinvention of government" initiative, great stress was placed on doing things more efficiently with fewer resources. Although restructuring under Atwood has achieved a more clear and limited set of objectives as well as some reorganization by downsizing, the fact remains that these efforts have fallen short of its initial intentions. In some sense, the restructuring effort has been negligible because the agency continues to use foreign aid mainly to promote U.S. businesses in the developing world. Although USAID is a component of U.S. foreign policy and exists partly to promote its interests, the humanitarian aspect and rhetoric about sustained development simply take a backseat. Furthermore, the agency is only quasi-independent because it remains subservient to the political mission of the State Department.

Under the current anti-aid climate, USAID has been on the defensive, justifying aid dollars by showing how it benefits or returns directly to U.S. citizens. Whereas in the past "pushing the money" was the only measure of success, today there are other measures, such as past performance. But USAID is still making the same mistakes.

Although the "reengineering" process has resulted in some streamlining, transforming it into a "high-performance, results-driven organization" has not materialized. For instance, there have been major obstacles in deploying the Integrated Management System, which was intended to link the agency's accounting, budget, personnel, procurement, and program operations into a single network. By 1998, the cost had exceeded $80 million and the system was not yet operational.

Finally, in trying to "reinvent" itself or "reengineer" its way of doing business, the agency is faced with a dilemma. "Reinventing government" emphasizes "partnership" with clients (contractors), which means working together. Putting it into practice makes these contractors "insiders" who have an advantage. Having been included in the restructuring process, a group of established insiders have an edge in being awarded the most lucrative contracts. The past performance process has little effect if the incumbent always has the advantage in being awarded a contract. The conclusion from the preceding discussion is that the "reinvention" effort has failed to achieve its desired objectives, if performance outcome is one of the measuring sticks. Furthermore, despite the reengineering effort that has been under way since 1994, the agency has not yet completed the organizational structure, systems, or procedures to make this work effectively.

The shift in aid practices because of privatization has made the government aid program increasingly commercialized. The current commercialization of aid does not reduce conflicting self-interested policies. Development aid projects and programs are now commercially linked to promote the financial interest of donors and their aid-reliant consulting clients that have a home constituency. As the ideology of the free market has gained ground, the key dimensions of aid have been left to influential private for-profit contractors to carry much of the development effort. USAID no longer does development projects; it just funds them. As a result, USAID has become a fund-dispensing agency providing a marginal management role and relying almost exclusively on contractors and grantees (NGOs) to do the work. From the point of view of the agency, under the present situation, this is a "positive sum game" in which all participants gain. However, in a market-based competitive situation private firms are more concerned about maximizing profit than in promoting sustainable development.

The conclusion is not that market forces are unimportant. They are. The essential point is that the use of contractors to channel foreign aid is an arrangement that benefits mainly private firms awarded contracts.

One of the intended tasks of privatization has been the promotion of the market to reduce costs and attain efficiency. This has not yet been achieved. In fact, the tendency has been to make competition more uneven. If the focus was originally cost-efficiency and effectiveness, the data indicate that the agency has not succeeded: contractors who are awarded mainly CPFF (level-of-effort) type contracts have only performed at an average level. Cost savings have not been substantial, and enhanced performance of contracts has not occurred. If the Federal Acquisition Streamlining Act (FASA) of 1994 established past performance as a key factor to be considered in the evaluation process to determine that the offeror will successfully perform the contract awarded, there are still deficiencies.

Past performance, as Bodenheimer (1997) puts it, has been revived "as a part of a broad initiative to commercialize the federal procurement process." But as mentioned previously, there are risks associated with past performance because many parts of the new regulations and politics remain controversial, undefined, and are left to the subjectivity of contracting officers and for the contractor to rebut when the contractor disagrees with the score given. Moreover, using the data in source selection is controversial, as are issues related to the interpretation of what is relevant data and assessing that data.

In one sense, there is no question that some activities currently undertaken by USAID could be better managed under contract, but contracting in its present form does not appear to be a precise solution to the problems of managing foreign aid because of the uncertain market environment, the lack of accountability on the part of contractors, and the system that favors the incumbent over new entrants. The evidence presented here offers only a partial view, but the results show some of the deficiencies with the type of contracts awarded at USAID and the performance outcome of such contracts. Although the initiatives taken to improve performance-based management at USAID have potential for improving the performance outcome of its programs, the agency is still undergoing a process of learning by doing. Performance-based contracting has devised ways to use more incentive-type contracts, but the agency has been very slow in adjusting to this recommendation.

THE OPTIONS AHEAD

Having examined the types of contracts in use by USAID in government-firm contracting, some of the options ahead as recommended by the author would be:

- Fixed-price type of contracts should be encouraged for the purchase of goods and incentive-type contracts for the acquisition of services. These contracts are preferable because often they can achieve significant cost savings to the government, are more appropriate for the type of work USAID does, and achieve better results.

- USAID should further streamline the procurement process. Although there are fewer contracts, they are being awarded mainly to the largest contractors for larger sums of money. This is not spurring procurement reforms was intended by NPR, but is making competition more uneven. The procurement process should be simplified and less expensive so that small- and medium-sized firms have a better chance winning contracts. The agency should make the procurement process more open because the process favors the incumbent and discriminates against newcomers.

- Although this is a requirement in the FAR, the Agency should not allow private contractors to challenge the past performance scores to the extent that it does at present. Judgments about performance are made by COTRs and are written out by the contracting officer who is directly engaged and following the project. Why should contractors be consulted?

- The agency does not seem to be doing enough about non-performers. Contractors who receive poor evaluations should not receive new contracts. In cases where contractors score well in some projects and poorly in others, the agency should step up its evaluation and monitoring process and be selective in awarding new contracts. If a large contractor consistently performs poorly in a specific area, it should not win more contracts in that area. One of the problems in evaluating performance has been that the technical officers are unwilling to give a contractor a poor performance rating because it reflects on the technical officers. On the other side, few contracting officers know what is going on with the contractor.

• Contractors who have ongoing contracts with USAID should not be awarded contracts to evaluate other contractors. The issue of treating contractors as "partners" has to be clarified. There is presently a conflict of interest when some contractors are "insiders" participating directly in activities that are best suited for the agency to do. USAID considers contractors "partners" even though they have a different agenda that is frequently incompatible with the promotion of sustainable development. Treating the contractor as a partner should not give the contractor and advantage for future work.

• Performance-based contracting has been promulgated as a way of simplifying SOW to make the contracting process more specific, efficient, and less costly. The bottom line is results. The agency doesn't tell contractors how to do their jobs, it just tells them the results it wants. Although the recommendations call for a more aggressive strategy to identify measurable results, it is still too early to fully assess the process.

• The contracting process of large contracts as administered by USAID puts only 25 percent of weight on the selection based on cost and 75 percent on the technical content of the proposal. This procedure tends to favor the larger, more established firms that can assemble a technical team of accountants, auditors, lawyers, engineers, and economists to write the proposal. Smaller firms, even if they have the "experts" in the field where the project is to be implemented, are at a disadvantage because they do not have all the resources it takes to put together a sophisticated proposal. One of the central goals of privatization is cost reduction, but this system puts very little emphasis on cost. The ratio should be more balanced.

• Solicit more contracts from firms in LDCs. The current system of using mainly U.S. contractors often fails to develop local expertise and keeps most of the aid money out of the local economy. The priority of channeling aid through contracts favors donor commercial interests and undermines local LDC capacity. Contracting relies on U.S. consultants, and accountability is not to the locals but to USAID, which is often powerless to do anything if the program or project goes awry.

Appendix

Appendix
USAID Contracts

CONTRACT	CONTRACT VALUE	AWARD DATE	COMPLETION DATE	CONTRACT TYPE	QUALITY	COST	ON TIME	USAID SATISFACT.	LDC SATISFACT.	MEAN SCORE	TYPE
1	$5,776	06.15.92	09.30.95	2	4.0	3.0	3.0	3.0	3.0	3.2	2
2	$10,390	04.01.94	08.15.95	2	4.0	3.0	3.0	4.0	4.0	3.8	2
3	$1,569	08.16.92	08.15.95	2	4.0	3.0	3.0	4.0	4.0	3.6	2
4	$1,099	08.01.92	10.31.95	2	4.0	3.0	3.0	4.0	4.0	3.8	2
5	$805	11.07.94	01.31.96	2	4.0	4.0	4.0	4.0	3.0	3.8	2
6	$140	05.05.95	08.27.95	5	4.0	4.0	3.0	3.0	4.0	3.6	1
7	$39,421	05.12.94	11.30.96	1	4.0	3.0	2.0	3.0	4.0	3.6	1
8	$2,813	03.14.94	09.13.97	2	3.0	3.0	4.0	3.0	3.4	3.2	2
9	$559	02.23.96	06.30.96	1	4.0	4.0	4.0	3.0	3.0	3.2	1
10	$6,627	10.29.92	08.31.95	2	4.0	3.0	3.0	5.0	4.0	4.0	2
11	$24,976	09.28.90	09.27.95	2	4.0	5.0	5.0	5.0	5.0	3.4	1
12	$2,783	07.21.91	07.20.95	2	4.0	4.0	3.0	3.0	3.0	4.8	2
13	$2,277	02.02.92	09.30.95	2	3.0	5.0	2.0	3.0	3.0	3.4	2
14	$1,240	03.25.92	07.17.95	2	4.0	4.0	4.0	4.0	3.0	3.2	2
15	$559	02.23.96	06.30.96	1	4.0	4.0	4.0	5.0	3.0	3.8	1
16	$15,000	06.14.96	09.27.96	1	4.0	3.0	5.0	4.0	3.0	4.0	1
17	$4,749	07.17.92	07.16.95	2	1.0	1.0	2.0	2.0	3.0	3.8	2
18	$500	09.28.95	09.28.96	5	4.0	3.0	4.0	4.0	4.0	1.8	1
19	$2,813	03.14.94	09.13.97	3	3.0	4.0	4.0	4.0	3.0	3.8	2
20	$13,977	01.10.94	01.10.98	2	4.0	4.0	3.5	5.0	3.5	3.4	2
21	$13,942	05.09.90	08.31.95	2	5.0	5.0	4.0	5.0	4.0	4.0	2
22	$23,550	05.07.93	05.31.96	2	4.5	4.0	3.5	4.0	5.0	4.6	2
23	$33,612	11.22.88	12.31.96	2	5.0	5.0	4.0	3.0	2.0	4.2	2
24	$6,020	10.31.88	12.30.96	2	4.0	5.0	3.0	4.0	4.0	3.6	2
25	$11,100	01.01.92	12.31.96	2	3.0	4.0	3.0	4.0	3.5	4.0	2
26	$5,700	11.18.91	07.15.95	2	4.0	4.0	4.0	3.0	4.0	3.5	2
27	$16,906	05.22.92	03.30.96	2	4.0	1.0	4.0	4.0	4.0	4.0	2
28	$16,263	06.20.91	10.19.96	4	4.0	3.0	3.0	3.0	4.0	3.0	2
29	$1,715	03.01.93	02.28.97	6	3.0	2.5	3.0	4.0	2.5	3.6	1
30	$3,747	09.16.94	02.28.97	2	3.0	4.0	2.0	3.0	3.0	2.6	2
31	$1,648	03.01.93	03.03.97	6	3.0	3.0	2.0	3.5	3.0	2.9	1

Appendix
USAID Contracts

CONTRACT	CONTRACT VALUE	AWARD DATE	COMPLETION DATE	CONTRACT TYPE	QUALITY	COST	ON TIME	USAID SATISFACT.	LDC SATISFACT.	MEAN SCORE	TYPE
32	$22,100	07.24.90	01.23.97	2	4.0	3.0	3.0	4.0	4.0	3.6	2
33	$6,815	09.24.90	07.15.97	2	3.0	4.0	3.0	3.0	4.0	3.4	2
34	$792	04.18.95	03.31.97	2	2.0	4.0	1.0	3.0	3.0	2.6	2
35	$21,285	10.21.93	07.31.97	2	3.0	3.1	3.1	2.5	3.2	3.0	2
36	$10,181	09.20.90	09.28.97	5	3.0	3.0	3.0	3.0	3.0	3.0	1
37	$125	10.16.95	06.30.97	2	4.0	4.0	3.0	4.0	4.0	3.8	2
38	$566	09.30.96	03.29.97	6	3.0	3.0	3.0	4.0	3.0	3.2	1
39	$15,760	06.26.92	07.26.96	2	3.0	3.0	3.0	3.0	3.0	3.0	2
40	$1,920	09.12.92	09.30.95	2	4.0	3.0	3.0	4.0	4.0	3.6	2
41	$1,348	03.01.94	09.30.96	2	3.0	3.0	3.0	4.0	3.0	3.0	2
42	$471	02.28.97	05.21.97	2	2.0	3.0	3.0	2.0	2.0	2.4	2
43	$740	09.02.94	09.01.96	1	4.0	3.0	4.0	4.0	4.0	3.8	1
44	$3,993	03.18.14	03.17.97	2	4.0	3.0	4.0	3.0	5.0	3.8	2
45	$11,101	01.01.92	12.31.96	2	3.0	4.0	3.0	4.0	3.5	3.5	2
46	$1,968	07.01.93	07.31.96	2	4.0	3.0	3.0	4.0	3.0	3.4	2
47	$1,799	02.07.94	04.30.97	2	3.5	3.0	2.5	3.5	3.5	3.2	2
48	$14,641	10.01.93	09.30.98	3	3.0	4.0	3.0	4.0	3.0	3.4	1
49	$9,148	11.22.88	12.31.96	2	5.0	4.0	4.0	3.0	2.0	3.6	2
50	$3,159	10.30.95	10.30.97	3	3.0	2.0	2.0	4.0	4.0	3.0	1
51	$746	09.01.95	08.31.97	2	5.0	2.0	5.0	3.7	4.0	3.7	2
52	$1,348	03.01.94	09.30.96	2	3.0	3.0	3.0	3.0	3.0	3.0	2
53	$1,475	04.01.95	06.30.97	2	3.0	3.0	3.0	3.0	3.0	3.0	2
54	$1,293	06.06.94	02.28.96	2	2.6	2.0	2.0	2.0	2.0	2.1	2
55	$1,793	09.30.94	09.29.97	2	1.5	2.0	2.0	2.5	2.0	2.0	2
56	$8,158	09.28.94	09.28.97	2	3.0	3.0	3.0	3.0	3.0	3.0	2
57	$4,916	10.26.95	10.25.97	2	2.0	2.0	2.0	2.0	2.0	2.0	2
58	$559	02.26.96	06.30.96	1	4.0	4.0	4.0	5.0	3.0	4.0	1
59	$5,500	04.01.94	03.31.97	2	3.0	4.0	3.0	3.0	4.0	3.4	2
60	$688	09.30.95	09.30.97	1	4.0	3.0	4.0	5.0	4.0	4.0	1
61	$2,300	09.20.93	03.31.97	2	3.0	3.0	3.0	3.0	3.0	3.0	2
62	$6,247	01.06.97	06.06.97	1	4.0	3.0	4.0	4.0	3.0	3.6	1

CONTRACT	CONTRACT VALUE	AWARD DATE	COMPLETION DATE	CONTRACT TYPE	QUALITY	COST	ON TIME	USAID SATISFACT.	LDC SATISFACT.	MEAN SCORE	TYPE
63	$14,059	05.17.95	09.30.97	3	4.0	5.0	4.0	5.0	4.0	4.4	1
64	$30,000	05.30.97	10.01.97	1	5.0	3.0	5.0	4.0	4.0	4.2	1
65	$249	06.26.96	02.28.97	6	5.0	4.0	4.0	5.0	5.0	4.6	1
66	$2,807	10.16.95	08.30.97	1	3.5	3.5	4.0	3.0	3.5	3.5	1
67	$5,889	01.10.95	01.09.98	2	4.0	2.0	3.0	4.0		3.2	2
68	$11,696	05.16.96	07.31.98	2	3.0	4.0	3.0	4.0		3.4	2
69	$12,269	11.15.94	08.14.98	2	4.0	3.0	3.0	4.0	3.0	3.4	2
70	$39,421	05.12.96	11.30.96	1	4.0	3.0	2.0	3.0	3.0	3.2	1
71	$16,612	09.27.94	06.25.96	1	3.0	3.0	3.0	3.0		3.0	4
72	$2,949	06.21.95	06.30.98	2	3.0	3.0	3.0	4.0	3.0	3.0	2
73	$2,312	02.21.95	07.15.97	2	3.0	4.0	2.0	3.0	3.0	3.4	2
74	$5,971	02.18.94	09.30.97	2	4.0	3.0	2.0	4.0	4.0	3.4	2
75	$709	02.21.95	03.31.98	2	3.0	4.0	3.0	3.0	3.0	3.2	2
76	$4,171	09.21.95	09.30.97	2	1.0	3.0	2.0	2.0	2.0	2.0	2
77	$138	09.30.96	01.31.97	2	3.0	3.0	3.0	4.0	3.0	3.2	2
78	$1,172	01.01.97	08.30.97	5	3.0	3.0	3.0	3.0	4.0	3.2	1
79	$2,400	02.03.94	12.31.96	5	4.0		3.0	4.0	4.0	3.8	1
80	$30,000	05.30.97	10.01.97	1	5.0		5.0	4.0	4.0	4.2	2
81	$720	02.25.94	02.28.98	2	4.0	3.0	3.0	4.0	4.0	3.6	1
82	$4,187	09.25.95	09.24.98	7	4.0	3.0	3.0	4.0	3.0	3.4	2
83	$5,369	03.09.95	03.05.98	2	3.0	3.0	3.0	3.0	3.0	3.0	1
84	$1,058	09.29.95	10.29.96	6	3.0	3.0	3.0	3.0	3.0	3.0	2
85	$4,956	06.30.96	07.30.97	6	3.0	4.0	3.0	4.0	3.0	3.4	1
86	$2,464	09.16.96	09.30.97	5	4.0	4.0	4.0	4.0	5.0	4.2	1
87	$3,949	08.07.96	02.28.97	6	3.0	4.0	4.0	3.0	3.0	3.2	1
88	$4,609	09.29.95	03.31.97	6	3.0	3.0	3.0	3.0	3.0	3.2	1
89	$4,956	06.30.96	07.30.97	6	3.0	4.0	3.0	4.0	3.0	3.4	1
90	$898	07.05.95	09.30.97	4	3.0	3.0	2.0	3.0	3.0	2.8	1
91	$2,684	07.11.96	07.10.98	2	5.0	5.0	5.0	4.0	4.0	4.6	3
92	$3,311	08.16.96	08.15.98	2	3.0	3.0	5.0	3.0	4.0	3.2	2
93	$974	02.19.93	04.15.97	5	3.0	3.0	3.0	4.0	3.0	3.2	1

Appendix
USAID Contracts

CONTRACT	CONTRACT VALUE	AWARD DATE	COMPLETION DATE	CONTRACT TYPE	QUALITY	COST	ON TIME	USAID SATISFACT.	LDC SATISFACT.	MEAN SCORE	TYPE
94	$16,670	07.21.92	07.16.98	2	4.0	4.0	3.0	4.0	4.0	3.8	2
95	$4,377	10.01.93	09.30.97	2	4.0	3.0	4.0	4.0	4.0	3.6	2
96	$4,622	09.01.93	12.31.98	2	3.0	3.0	3.0	3.0	4.0	3.2	2
97	$12,612	09.30.92	09.29.97	2	5.0	4.0	4.0	4.0	4.0	4.2	2
98	$1,493	12.23.93	09.29.97	2	3.0	2.0	2.0	2.0	3.0	2.3	2
99	$53,487	09.24.93	09.22.97	2	4.0	3.0	3.0	4.0	3.0	3.4	2
100	$22,100	07.24.90	01.23.98	2	4.0	3.0	3.0	4.0	4.0	3.6	2
101	$13,969	12.20.93	06.30.98	2	3.0	2.0	3.0	3.0	3.0	2.8	2
102	$3,509	04.13.92	12.31.95	2	5.0	4.0	4.0	4.0	4.0	4.2	2
103	$1,373	09.29.92	09.29.96	7	3.0	3.0	3.0	4.0	4.0	3.4	1
104	$4,999	05.01.93	04.30.98	2	3.0	1.0	2.0	3.0	4.0	2.6	2
105	$9,798	09.28.90	09.29.96	2	3.0	3.0	3.0	3.0	3.0	3.0	2
106	$11,605	12.09.92	09.30.98	2	4.0	3.0	3.0	3.0	4.0	3.4	2
107	$7,464	01.28.93	08.26.97	2	4.0	4.0	3.0	4.0	4.0	3.8	2
108	$11,251	03.01.93	07.31.97	2	3.0	3.0	2.7	3.3	3.0	3.0	2
109	$3,247	05.30.91	06.30.98	2	4.0	4.0	4.0	4.0	4.0	4.0	2
110	$5,639	06.26.92	10.26.96	2	3.0	3.0	3.0	3.0	3.0	3.0	2
111	$1,968	07.01.93	07.31.96	2	4.0	3.0	3.0	4.0	3.0	3.4	2
112	$6,292	03.29.93	03.28.97	2	3.0	3.0	3.0	2.0	2.0	2.6	2
113	$3,485	10.01.92	09.30.96	2	3.0	3.0	4.0	3.0	3.0	3.2	2
114	$3,835	06.08.92	09.30.97	2	4.0	3.0	4.0	4.0	3.0	3.6	2
115	$8,075	11.30.91	07.31.97	2	4.0	3.0	4.0	4.0	3.0	3.6	2
116	$12,589	09.28.90	09.30.97	2	3.0	4.0	3.0	4.0	4.0	3.6	2

Source: Past Performance Reports, Division of Procurement, USAID.

Glossary of Acronyms

AIDAR	U.S. Agency for International Development Acquisition Regulation
CO	Contracting Officer
CBD	*Commerce Business Daily*
CP	Cost-Plus or Cost-Reimbursement
COTR	Contracting Officer Technical Representative
CPFF	Cost-Plus Fixed Fee
CRS	Congressional Research Service
DAC	Development Assistance Committee
ERP	Economic Recovery Program (Marshall Plan)
FAR	Federal Acquisition Regulations
FASA	Federal Acquisition Streamlining Act
FP	Fixed-Price
FY	Fiscal Year
GAO	General Accounting Office
GNP	Gross National Product
GPRA	Government Performance and Results Act
GSA	General Services Administration
IC	Incentive-type Contracts
IDRC	International Development Research Centre
IFB	Invitation for Bids
IQC	Indefinite Quantity Contracts
LDCs	Less Developed Countries
LOE	Level-of-Effort Contracts
NGO	Non-Governmental Organizations
NICs	Newly Industrializing Countries
NIS	Newly Independent States (of the former Soviet Union)
NPR	National Performance Review
ODA	Official Development Assistance

OECD	Organization for Economic Cooperation for Development
OFPP	Office of Federal Procurement Policy
OMB	Office of Management and Budget
PBC	Performance-Based Contracting
PVO	Private Voluntary Organizations
RFP	Request for Proposal
SAREC	Swedish Agency of Research Cooperation with Developing Countries
SOW	Statement of Work
USAID	United States Agency for International Development
UN	United Nations
UNCTAD	United Nations Commission on Trade and Development
US	United States
UNDP	United Nations Development Program

Bibliography

Aktan, Coscun Can. "An Introduction to the Theory of Privatization." *Journal of Social, Political and Economic Studies* 20, (Summer 1995): 187-215.

Alston, Frank M., Margaret M. Worthington, and Louis P. Goldsman. *Contracting with the Federal Government*. New York: John Wiley & Sons, 1992.

Ascher, Kate. *The Politics of Privatization: Contracting Out Public Services*. New York: St. Martin's Press, 1989.

Atlantic Management Center. *Performance-Based Contracting. Participant's Manual.* U.S. Agency for International Development, Office of Procurement, June 1997.

Atwood, Brian. "Statement of J. Brian Atwood, Administrator of USAID to the Subcommittee on International Operations, Committee on Foreign Relations, U.S. Senate, Washington, D.C., 11 May, 1995.

Bailey, Elizabeth, and Janet Rothenberg, (ed.) *The Political Economy of Privatization and Deregulation*. Aldershot, England: Edward Elgar Publishing Co., 1995.

Baker, Keith L., William A. Erie, and Scott J. Parkinson. *Financial Issues for the Contracts Professional*. Washington, D.C.: National Contract Management Association, 1993.

Baldwin, David A. *Economic Statecraft*. Princeton: Princeton University Press, 1985.

Bauer, Peter, and Basil Yamey. "Foreign Aid: What Is at Stake?" *The Public Interest* 68 (Summer 1982): 53-69.

Baye, Michael R., and Richard O. Beil. *Managerial Economics and Business Strategy.* Boston: Irwin, 1994.

Beausoleil, Joseph. "Contractor Performance Evaluations—An Effective Contract Administration Tool," *Contract Management* (October 1997): 39-41.

Bennett, James T., and Manuel H. Johnson. *Better Government at Half Price: Private Production of Public Services.* Ottawa: Caroline House Publishers, 1981.

Berg, Elliot J. "Recent Trends and Issues in Development Strategies and Development Assistance." In *From Transformation to Cooperation? U.S. and Soviet Aid to Developing Countries,* edited by Richard Feinberg and Ratchik M. Avokov. New Brunswick, N.J.: Transaction Publishers, 1991.

———. *Rethinking Technical Cooperation.* New York: Regional Bureau for Africa, United Nations Development Programme and Development Alternatives, 1993.

———. "Dilemmas in Donor Aid Strategies." In *Perspectives on Aid and Development,* edited by Catherine Gwin and Joan M. Nelson. Washington, D.C.: Overseas Development Council, Policy Essay No. 22, 1997: 79-94.

Berger, Renee A. "Private Sector Initiatives in the Reagan Era: New Actors Rework an Old Theme." In *The Reagan Presidency and the Governing of America,* edited by Lester M. Salomon and Michael S. Lund. Washington, D.C.: Urban Institute Press, 1985.

Berkman, Steve. "The Impact of Corruption on Technical Cooperation Projects in Africa," *International Journal of Technical Cooperation* 2, (Winter 1996): 209-223.

Bocherding, Thomas E. "Towards a Positive Theory of Public Sector Supply Arrangements." Discussion paper 79-15-3. Burnaby, B.C., Simon Fraiser University, 1979.

Bodenheimer, David Z. "Past Performance: The Sequel," National Contract Management Association, Topical Issues in Procurement Series 8, No. 3 (September 1997): 1-8.

Boone, Peter. "Politics and the Effectiveness of Aid." Discussion Paper 272, Centre for Economic Performance, London School of Economics, December 1995.

Borland, Jeff. "On Contracting Out: Some Labor Market Considerations." *Australian Economic Review,* 107 (July-September 1994): 86-90.

Boston, Jonathan. "Purchasing Policy Advice: The Limits of Contracting Out." *Governance: An International Journal of Policy and Administration* 7, (January 1994): 1-30.

———. "Inherently Governmental Functions and the Limits of Contracting Out." In *The State Under Contract,* edited by J. Boston 78-111. Wellington, New Zealand: Bridget Williams Books, 1995.

Brautingam, Deborah. *Chinese Aid and African Development.* New York: St. Martin's Press, 1998.

Brown, William Adams, Jr., and Redvers Opie. *American Foreign*

Assistance. Washington, D.C.: Brookings Institution, 1953.

Browne, Stephen. *Foreign Aid in Practice.* London: Frances Pinter Publishers, 1990.

Bruno, Marta. "Playing the Cooperation game: Strategies Around International Aid in Post-Socialist Russia." In *Surviving Post-Socialism: Local Strategies and Regional Responses in Eastern Europe and the Former Soviet Union*, edited by Sue Bridger and Frances Pine. London: Routledge, 1998.

Buchanan, James M. "Why Does Government Grow?" In *Budgets and Bureaucrats: The Sources of Government Growth*, edited by Thomas Bocherding. Durham: Duke University Press, 1977.

Burman, Allan. "Putting Past Performance First." *Contract Management* (October 1997): 37-38.

Burnside, Craig, and David Dollar. "Aid, Policies, and Growth." World Bank working paper 1777, Policy Research Department, June 1997.

Business Alliance for International Economic Development. *Foreign Assistance: What's in it for Americans?* Washington, D.C., June 1996.

Butler, Stuart. "Changing the Political Dynamics of Government." In *Prospects for Privatization*, edited by Steve H. Hanke. New York: Academy of Political Science, 1987.

———."Privatization for Public Purposes." In *Privatization and its Alternatives*, edited by William T. Gormley 17-24. Madison: University of Wisconsin Press, 1991.

Carroll, James D., A. Lee Fritschler, and Bruce L. R. Smith. "Supply-Side Management in the Reagan Administration." *Public Administration Review* 45 (November-December 1985): 805-814.

Carver, Robert H. "Examining the Premises of Contracting Out." *Public Productivity and Management Review* 13, (Fall 1989): 27-40.

Cason, Jim. "The U.S. Backing Out of Africa." *Review of African Political Economy* 71 (March 1997): 147-153.

Cassen, Robert, and Associates. *Does Aid Work?* Oxford: Clarendon Press, 1986.

Choate, Pat. *Agents of Influence.* New York: A. A. Knoff, 1990.

Cibinic, John, and Ralph C. Nash. *Cost Reimbursement Contracting.* Washington, D.C.: National Law Center, Government Contracts Program, George Washington University, 1993.

———. *Formation of Government Contracts.* 3rd ed. Washington, D.C.: National Law Center, The Government Contracts Program, George Washington University, 1998.

Commission on International Development (Pearson) *Partners in Development.* London: Pall Mall Press, 1969.

Congressional Budget Office. *The Role of Foreign Aid in Development.*

Washington, D.C.: Congress of the United States, Congressional Budget Office, May 1997.

Congressional Research Service. *The Private Enterprise Initiative of the Agency for International Development.* Report Prepared for the Committee of Foreign Affairs, U.S. House of Representatives, 1989

——. *U.S. Foreign Aid in a Changing World: Options for New Priorities.* Report prepared for the Subcommittee on Europe and the Middle East, U.S. Committee on Foreign Affairs, U.S. House of Representatives, February 1991.

Conteh-Morgan, Earl. American Foreign Aid and Global Power Projection: The Geopolitics of Resource Allocation, Aldershot, England: Darmouth Publishing Co., 1990.

Corwin, Julie. "Playing the AID Game," *U.S. News & World Report*, 3 October, 1994

Crawford, Gordon. "Foreign Aid and Political Conditionality: Issues of Effectiveness and Consistency." *Democratization* 4 (Autumn 1997): 69-105.

Crook, Mike. "The Lamb Lies Down with the Lion: The Privatization of Aid and NGOs." *Development Bulletin* 38 (July 1996): 25-27.

Curti, Merle, and Kendall Birr. *Prelude to Point Four: American Technical Missions Overseas, 1838-1938.* Madison: University of Wisconsin Press, 1954.

Deady, Tim. "Government Contracting Up 11.3% Here." *Washington Business Journal*, 7 April 1997: 1-3.

DeHoog, Ruth. *Contracting Out for Human Services.*. Albany: State University of New York Press, 1984.

Development Assistance Committee. *United States.* Paris: OECD, Development Cooperation Review Series No 28, 1998.

Development Committee. *Aid for Development: The Key Issues.* Washington, D.C.: World Bank and International Monetary Fund, 1986.

Domberger, Simon. "Public Sector Contracting: Does it Work?" *Australian Economic Review* 107 (July-September 1994) : 91-96.

Domberger, Simon, and Stephen Rimmer. "Competitive Tendering and Contracting Out in the Public Sector: A Survey." *Journal of the Economics of Business* (December 1994): 439-453.

Domberger, Simon, and Paul Jensen. "Contracting Out by the Public Sector: Theory, Evidence, Prospects." *Oxford Review of Economic Policy* 13, No 4, (1997): 67-78.

Donahue, John D. *The Privatization Decision: Public Ends, Private Means.* New York: Basic Books, 1989.

Downs, George H., and Patrick D. Larkey. *The Search for Government*

Efficiency: From Hubris to Helplessness. New York: Random House, 1986.

Eaton, Leslie. "Public Money Foots the Bill for 'Privatized' Foreign Aid." *New York Times*, 7 February 1996, A1, C21.

Edwards, Vernon J. *How to Evaluate Past Performance: A Best Value Approach.* Washington, D.C.: Government Contracts Program, George Washington University, 1995).

Epstein, Paul D. "Measuring the Performance of Public Services," In *Public Productivity Handbook*, edited by Marc Halzer. New York: Marcel Bekker, 1992.

Epstein, Susan B., Larry Q. Nowels, and Steven A. Hildreth. *Foreign Policy Agency Reorganization in the 105th Congress*, Washington, D.C.: Congressional Research Service, Library of Congress, CRS Report for Congress, 6 November 1998.

Fanning, Marina. "A Contractor's View: Performance-Based Contracting." *On Track* 2, (July/August 1996): 1-3.

FAR. *Federal Acquisition Regulation.* Chicago: CCH, 1997.

Ferris, James M., and Elizabeth Graddy. "Contracting Out: For What? With Whom?" *Public Administration Review* 46, No 4 (1986): 332-344.

———. "Production Costs, Transaction Costs, and Local Government Contractor Choice." *Economic Inquiry* XXIX (July 1991): 541-554.

Fitzgerald, Randall. *When Government Goes Private: Successful Alternatives to Public Services.* New York: Universe Books, 1988.

Frederickson, George. "Comparing the Reinvention of Government with the New Public Administration." *Public Administration Review* 56 (May-June 1996): 263-270.

GAO. *Government Contracting: A Proposal for a Program to Study the Profitability of Government Contracts*, Washington, D.C.: U.S. General Accounting Office, GAO/NSIAD-87-175, September 1987.

———. *Civilian Agency Procurement: Improvements Needed in Contracting and Contract Administration.* Washington, D.C.: General Accounting Office, GAO/GGD-89-109, 5 September, 1989.

———. *AID Can Improve its Management of Overseas Contracting.* Washington, D.C.: U.S. General Accounting Office, GAO/NSIAD-91-31, October 1990.

———. *AID Can Improve its Management and Oversight of Host Country Contracts.* Washington, D.C.: U.S. General Accounting Office, GAO/NSIAD-91-108, May 1991a.

———. *Foreign Assistance: AID's Use of Personal Services Contracts Overseas.* Washington, D.C.: U.S. General Accounting Office, GAO/NSIAD-91-237, September 1991b.

———. *Foreign Assistance: AID's Use of Personal Service Contracts*

Overseas. U.S. General Accounting Office, GAO/NSIAD-91-237, 13 September, 1991c.

——. *Management Problems Persist at AID.* Washington, D.C.: U.S. General Accounting Office, GAO/NSIAD-92-31, 1 May 1992a.

——. *Foreign Assistance: A Profile of the Agency for International Development.* Washington, D.C.: U.S. General Accounting Office, GAO/NSIAD-92-148, 3 April, 1992b.

——. *Aid Management: Strategic Management Can Help AID Face Current and Future Challenges.* Washington, D.C.: U.S. General Accounting Office, GAO/NSIAD-92-100, March 1992c.

——. *Foreign Assistance: AID's Private Sector Assistance Program at a Crossroads.* Washington, D.C.: U.S. General Accounting Office, GAO/NSIAD-93-55, December 1992d.

——. *Foreign Economic Assistance Issues,* Washington, D.C.: U.S. General Accounting Office, GAO/OCG-93-25TR, December 1992e.

——. *Foreign Assistance: AID Strategic Direction and Continued Management Improvements Needed,* Washington, D.C.: U.S. General Accounting Office, GAO/NSIAD-93-106, 11 June, 1993.

——. *AID's Indefinite Contracts Assist Privatization Efforts but Lack Adequate Oversight.* Washington, D.C.: U.S. General Accounting Office, GAO/NSIAD-94-61, January 1994.

——. *Foreign Assistance: Private Voluntary Organizations: Contributions and Limitations.* Washington, D.C.: U.S. General Accounting Office, GAO/NSIAD-96-36, December 1995b.

——. *Government Contracts: An Overview of the Federal Contracting Out Program,* Washington, DC: U.S. General Accounting Office, GAO/T-GGD-95-131, 29 March, 1995a.

——. *Status of USAID's Reforms.* Washington, D.C.: U.S. General Accounting Office. GAO/NSAID-96-241BR, September 1996a.

——. *Foreign Assistance: Harvard Institute for International Development's Work in Russia and the Ukraine.* Washington, D.C.: U.S. General Accounting Office. GAO/NSIAD-97-87, November 1996b.

Geddes, Barbara. "The Politics of Economic Liberalization." *Latin American Research Review* 30, No 2, (1995): 195-214.

Gore, Al. *Creating a Government that Works Better & Costs Less: Agency for International Development.* Accompanying Report of the National Performance Review, Office of the Vice President, Washington, D.C., September 1993.

Gormley, William T. "The Privatization Controversy." In *Privatization and its Alternatives*, edited by William T. Gormley. Madison: University of Wisconsin Press, 1991.

Gormley, William T., ed. *Privatization and its Alternatives.* Madison:

University of Wisconsin Press, 1991.

Grant, Richard, and Jan Nijman. "Foreign Aid at the End of the Century: The Emerging Transnational Order and the Crisis of Modernity," In *The Global Crisis in Foreign Aid*, edited by R. Grant and J. Nijman. Syracuse: Syracuse University Press, 1998.

Green, Duncan. *Silent Revolution: The Rise of Market Economies in Latin America*. London: Cassell, 1995.

Greene, Jeffrey D. "Does Privatization Make a Difference? The Impact of Private Contracting on Municipal Efficiency." *International Journal of Public Administration* 17, No 7 (1994): 1299-1325.

Griffin, Keith. "Foreign Aid After the Cold War." *Development and Change* 22, (October 1991): 645-684.

Guttman, Daniel. "Contracting for Government." Issue paper on "Making Reform Work," National Academy of Public Administration, January 1997.

Guttman, Daniel, and Barry Willner. *The Shadow of Government: The Government's Multibillion Dollar Giveaway of its Decision-Making to Private Management Consultants, "Experts," and their Think Tanks*, New York: Pantheon Books, 1976.

Hancock, Graham. *Lords of Poverty: The Power, Prestige, and Corruption of the International Aid Business*. New York: Atlantic Monthly Press, 1989.

Hanke, Steve H., and Barney Dowdle. "Privatizing the Public Domain." In *Prospects for Privatization*, edited by Steve H. Hanke, 111-123. New York: Academy of Political Science, 1987.

Hanrahan, John D. *Government by Contract*. New York: W. W. Norton & Co., 1983.

———. *Government for Sale*. Washington, D.C.: American Federation of State, County, and Municipal Workers, 1987.

Haugaard, Lisa. "Development Aid: Some Small Steps Forward." *NACLA Report on the Americas* 21 (September/October 1997): 29-33.

Hecht, James L. "Good Intentions: The Mismanagement of Foreign Aid." *Christian Century*, 6 November, 1996a: 1063-1065.

———. "Why AID's Programs Are Not Effective in Russia." Temple University, 1996b.

Herbst, Jeffrey. "The Politics of Privatization in Africa." In *The Political Economy of Public Sector Reform and Privatization*, edited by Suleiman and Waterbury. Boulder: Westview Press, 1990.

Hewitt, Adrian P., and Tony Killick. "Bilateral Aid Conditionality and Policy Leverage." In *Foreign Aid Towards the Year 2000: Experiences and Challenges*, edited by Olav Stokke, 130-167. London: Frank Cass, 1996.

Hiller, John R. and Robert D. Tollison. "Incentive Versus Cost-Plus Contracts in Defense Procurement." *Journal of Industrial Economics*, 26, (March 1978): 239-248.

Hirschman, Albert O. *Development Projects Observed.* Washington, DC: The Brookings Institution, 1967.

Hoben, Allan. "USAID: Organizational and Institutional Issues and Effectiveness," In *Cooperation for International Development: The United States and the Third World in the 1990s,* edited by Robert J. Berg and David Gordon, 253-278. Boulder: Lynne Rienner Publishers, 1989.

Holtz, Herman. *Government Contracts: Proposalmanship and Winning Strategies.* New York: Plenum Press, 1979.

Hook, Steven W. *National Interest and Foreign Aid.* Boulder: Lynne Rienner Publishers, 1995.

——. "Foreign Aid in a Transformed World." In *Foreign Aid Toward the Millenium,* edited by Steven W. Hook, 11-66. Boulder: Lynne Rienner, 1996.

Hough, Jerry F. *The Struggle for the Third World.* Washington, D.C.: Brookings Institution, 1986.

Hoy, Paula. *Players and Issues in International Aid.* West Hartford, Conn.: Kumarian Press, 1998.

Ikenberry, John. "The International Spread of Privatization Policies: Inducements, Learning, and Policy Bandwagoning." In *The Political Economy of Public Sector Reform and Privatization,* edited by Suleiman and Waterbury. Boulder: Westview Press, 1990.

IMF. *International Financial Statistics.* Washington, DC: International Monetary Fund, 1997.

Interaction. "10 Myths and Realities of Foreign Aid." Washington, D.C.: American Council for Voluntary Action, n.d.

Jepma, Catrinus J. *The Tying of Aid.* Paris: Organization for Economic Cooperation and Development, 1991.

——. *Inter-Nation Policy Co-ordination and Untying of Aid,* Aldershot, England: Avebury, 1994.

Kaplan, Sheila. "Porkbarrel Politics at USAID." *Multinational Monitor* 14 (September 1993): 10-15.

Kelman, Steven. *Procurement and Public Management: The Fear of Discretion and the Quality of Government Performance.* Washington, D.C.: EAI Press, 1990.

——. "Deregulating Federal Procurement: Nothing to Fear but Discretion Itself." In *Deregulating the Public Service: Can Government be Improved?,* edited by John DiIulio, 102-128. Washington, D.C.: Brookings Institution, 1994.

Kemp, R. L., ed. *Privatization: The Provision of Public Services by the Public Sector*. Jefferson, N.C.: McFarland and Co., 1991.

Kimaru, Christopher M. *International Charity for Self-Interest: U.S. Foreign Aid Policy Toward Tropical Africa in the 1980s*. Cammack, N.Y.: Nova Science Publishers, 1996.

King, Stephen P. "Competitive Tendering and Contracting Out: An Introduction." *Australian Economic Review*, 107 (July-September, 1994): 75-78.

Korten, David C. *Getting to the 21st Century: Voluntary Action and the Global Agenda*. West Hartford, Conn.: Kumarian Press, 1990.

Kraus, Melvin. *Development Without Aid*. Palo Alto: Hoover Institution Press, 1983.

Krueger, Anne O., Constantine Michalopoulos, and Vernon W. Ruttan. *Aid and Development*. Baltimore: Johns Hopkins University Press, 1989.

Kull, Steven. *American and Foreign Aid: A Study of American Public Attitudes*. Washington, D.C.: Center for International and security Studies at the University of Maryland, Program on International Policy Studies, 1995.

Kull, Steven, I. M. Destler, and Clay Ramsay. *The Foreign Policy Gap: How Policy Makers Missed the Public*. Washington, D.C.: Center for International and Security Studies at the University of Maryland, Program on International Policy Studies, October 1997.

Laurent, Anne. "Buying Smart." *Government Executive* 29, No. 4 (April 1997): 28-37.

Lebovic, James H. "National Interest and U.S. Foreign Aid: The Carter and Reagan Years." *Journal of Peace Research* 25, No 2 (1988): 115-135.

Lecomte, Bernard J. *Project Aid: Limitations and Alternatives*. Paris: Organization for Economic Cooperation and Development, 1986.

Lieberman, Ira. "Privatization in Latin America and Eastern Europe in the Context of Political and Economic Reform." *The World Economy* 17, (July 1994): 551-576.

Lopez-de-Silanes, Florencio, Andrei Shleifer and Robert W. Vishny. "Privatization in the United States." *Rand Journal of Economics* 28, (Autumn 1997): 447-471.

Lumsdaine, David Holloran. *Moral Vision in International Politics: The Foreign Aid Regime, 1949-1989*. Princeton: Princeton University Press, 1993.

MacManus, Susan A. *Doing Business with Government*. New York: Paragon House, 1992.

Management Concepts, Inc. *Types of Contracts*. Washington, D.C. 1990.

Maren, Michael. *The Road to Hell: The Ravaging Effects of Foreign Aid and*

International Charity. New York: Free Press, 1997.

Mazur, Laurie Ann, and Susan E. Sechler. "Global Interdependence and the Need for Social Stewardship." Global Interdependence Initiative, Rockefeller Brothers Fund, Paper No 1, 1997.

McAfee, Preston R. and McMillan, John. "Bidding for Contracts: The Principal-Agent Analysis." *Rand Journal of Economics* 17 (1986): 326-338.

——. *Incentives in Government Contracting*. Toronto: University of Toronto Press, 1988.

McCall, J. J. "The Simple Economics of Incentive Contracting." *American Economic Review* 60 (December 1970): 837-846.

McDaniel, John B. "Public Contracts: Statute Eases Certification Standards." *The National Law Journal* 27 May 1996.

McNeil, D. *The Contradictions of Foreign Aid*. London: Croom Helm, 1981.

Meier, G. M. "The New Political Economy and Policy Reform." *Journal of International Development* 5, No. 4 (1993): 381-389.

Mickelwait, D. R., D. F. Sweet, and E. P. Morss. *New Directions in Development: A Study of U.S. AID*. Boulder, Westview Press, 1979.

Millward, Robert. "The Comparative Performance of Public and Private Ownership." In *The Mixed Economy*, edited by E. Roll, 58-93. London: Macmillan Publishers, 1982.

Mitchell, William, and Randy Simmons. *Beyond Politics: Markets, Welfare, and the Failure of Bureaucracy*. Boulder: Westview Press, 1995.

Moon, Bruce E. *The Political Economy of Basic Human Needs*. Ithaca: Cornell University Press, 1991.

Moore, Frederick T. "Incentive Contracts." In *Defense Management*, edited by Stephen Enke, 213-231, Englewood Cliffs, N.J.: Prentice Hall, 1967.

Morrison, Elizabeth, and Randall B. Purcell, eds. *Players and Issues in U.S. Foreign Aid*. Hartford, Conn.: Kumarian Press, 1988.

Mosley, Paul. *Overseas Aid: Its Defense and Reform*. Brighton, England: Wheatsheaf Books, 1987.

Myers, Steven Lee. "AID Suspends Harvard Grant, Saying Money Was Misused." *New York Times*, 22 May 1997.

Nagle, James F. *How to Review a Federal Contract and Research Federal Contract Law*. Washington, D.C.: American Bar Association, 1990.

Nash, Ralph C., and John Cibinic. *Competitive Negotiation: The Source Selection Process*, Washington, D.C.: National Law Center, Government Contracts Program, George Washington University, 1993.

Nash, Ralph C., Steven N. Schooner, and Karen R. O'Brien. *The Government Contracts Reference Book: A Comprehensive Guide to the Language of Procurement*. Washington, D.C.: Law School, Government Contracts Program, George Washington University, 1998.

National Performance Review. *Agency for International Development*. Accompanying Report of the National Performance Review, Office of the Vice President, Washington, D.C., September 1993a.

———. *Reinventing Federal Procurement. Creating a Government that Works Better and Costs Less.* Accompanying Report of the National Performance Review, September 1993b.

Nelson, Joan, ed. *Economic Crisis and Policy Change: The Politics of Adjustment in the Third World.* Princeton: Princeton University Press, 1990.

Nkya, Estomih Jonas. "From Divestment to Public Sector Reform in Tanzania: Explaining Forms of Privatization as Policy Choice Options." Ph.D. Diss. Graduate School of Public and International Affairs, University of Pittsburgh, 1995.

Nowels, Larry Q., and Curt Tarnoff, *Foreign Assistance as an Instrument of U.S. Leadership Abroad.* Washington, D.C.: National Policy Association, 1997.

Office of Management and Budget. "Government-wide Guidance on Contract Administration." Memorandum for Agency Senior Procurement Executive, Washington, D.C.: Office of Federal Procurement Policy, 1991.

O'Hanlon, Michael, and Carol Graham. *A Half Penny on the Federal Dollar: The Future of Development Aid.* Washington, D.C.: Brookings Institution Press, 1997.

OMB-AID Swat Team. *Improving Management at the Agency for International Development.* Washington, D.C., 1992.

Organization for Economic Cooperation and Development (OECD). *Private Sector Development: A Guide to Donor Support.* Paris: Organization for Economic Cooperation and Development, 1995a.

———. *United States.* Development Cooperation Series, No. 8. Paris: Organization for Economic Cooperation and Development, 1995b.

Osborn, David, and Ted Gaebler. *Reinventing Government: The Entrepreneurial Spirit is Transforming the Public Sector.* Reading, Mass.: Addison-Wesley Publishing Co., 1992.

Overseas Development Institute. "NGOs and Official Donors." *Development Bulletin 38*, July 1996.

Pack, Janet Rothenberg. "The Opportunities and Constraints of Privatization." In *Privatization and its Alternatives*, edited by William T. Gormley. Madison: The University of Wisconsin Press, 1991.

Pastor, Robert A. *Congress and the Politics of United States Foreign Economic Policy.* Berkeley: University of California Press, 1980.

Pearson, Lester. *Partners in Development.* Washington, D.C.: USAID, 1969.

Porter, David. *U.S. Economic Foreign Aid: A Case Study of the United States*

Agency for International Development. New York: Garland Publishing, 1990.

Prager, Jonas. "Contracting Out: Theory and Policy," *Journal of International Law and Politics* 25 (Fall 1992): 73-111.

———. "Contracting Out Government Services: Lessons from the Private Sector." *Public Administration Review* 54, No. 2 (1994): 176-184.

Prager, Jonas and Swati Desai. "Privatizing Local Government Operations: Lessons from Federal Contracting Out Methodology." *Public Productivity and Management Review* 20 (December 1996): 185-203.

Quiggin, John. "The Fiscal Gains from Contracting Out: Transfers or Efficiency Improvements." *Australian Economic Review* 107 (July-September 1994): 97-101.

Rabe, Stephen G. *Eisenhower and Latin America: The Foreign Policy of Anti-Communism.* Chapel Hill: University of North Carolina Press, 1988.

Raffer, Kunibert, and Hans W. Singer. *The Foreign Aid Business: Economic Assistance and Development Cooperation.* Cheltenham, England: Edward Elgar, 1996.

Randel, Judith, and Tony German. *The Reality of Aid: An Independent Review of Development Cooperation.* London: Earthscan Publications, 1997.

Riddell, Roger C. *Foreign Aid Reconsidered.* Baltimore: Johns Hopkins University Press, 1987.

———. "The Moral Case for post-Cold War Development Aid." *International Journal* 51 (Spring 1996): 191-210.

Riemer, W. H. *Handbook of Government Contract Administration.* Englewood Cliffs, N.J.: Prentice Hall, 1968.

Rimmer, Stephen J. "Competitive Tendering and Contracting: Theory and Research." *Australian Economic Review* 107 (July-September 1994): 79-85.

Robbins, Carla Anne, and Steve Leisman. "How an Aid Program Vital to New Economy of Russia Collapsed." *The Wall Street Journal,* 13 August 1997, A1.

Robinson, Mark. "Privatising the Voluntary Sector: NGOs as Public Service Contractors." In *NGOs, States and Donors: Too Close to Comfort?*, edited by David Hulme and Michael Edwards. New York: St. Martin's Press, 1997.

Rondinelli, Dennis. *Development Administration and U.S. Foreign Aid Policy.* Boulder: Lynne Rienner Publishers, 1987.

———. "Reforming U.S. Foreign Aid Policy: Constraints on Development Assistance." *Policy Studies Journal* 18 (Fall 1989): 67-85.

Roth, Gabriel. *The Private Provision of Public Services in Developing Countries*. New York: Oxford University Press, 1987.

Ruttan, Vernon W. "Why Foreign Economic Assistance?" *Economic Development and Cultural Change* 37 (January 1989): 411-424.

——. *United States Development Assistance Policy: The Domestic Politics of Foreign Economic Aid*. Baltimore: Johns Hopkins University Press, 1996.

Savas, E. S. *Privatization: A Key to Better Government*. Chattam, N.J.: Chattam House Publishers, 1987.

Savoie, Donald J. *Thatcher, Reagan, Mulroney: In Search of a New Bureaucracy*. Pittsburgh: Pittsburgh University Press, 1994.

Saxby, John. "Who Owns the Private Aid Agencies?" In *Compassion and Calculation: The Business of Private Foreign Aid*, edited by David Sogge, 36-67. London: Pluto Press, 1996.

Scherer, F.M. "The Theory of Contractual Incentives for Cost reduction." *Quarterly Journal of Economics*, 78, (February 1964): 257-280.

Seidenstat, Paul. "Privatization: Trends, Interplay of Forces, and Lessons Learned." *Policy Studies Journal* 24, No 3 (1996): 464-477.

Serageldin, Ismail. *Development Partners: Aid and Cooperation in the 1990s*. Stockholm: Swedish International Development Authority, 1993.

Sewell, John W., and Christine E. Contee. "U.S. Foreign Aid in the 1980s: Reordering Priorities." In *International Political Economy: A Reader*, edited by Kendall W. Stiles and Tsuneo Akaha. New York: Harper Collins Publishers, 1991.

Sexton, Edwin A., and Terence N. Decker. "U.S. Foreign Aid: Is it for Friends, Development or Politics?" *Journal of Social, Political and Economic Studies*, 17 (1992): 303-315.

Sogge, David, and Simon Zadek. "Laws of the Market." In *Compassion and Calculation: The Business of Private Foreign Aid*, edited by David Sogge, 68-96. London: Pluto Press, 1996.

Starr, Paul. "The Limits of Privatization." In *Prospects for Privatization*, edited by Steve H. Hanke, 124-137. New York: The Academy of Political Science, 1987.

——. "The Meaning of Privatization." In *Privatization and the Welfare State*, edited by Sheila B. Kamerman and Alfred J. Kahn, 15-48. Princeton: Princeton University Press, 1989.

Stokke, Olav, ed. *Foreign Aid Towards the Year 2000*. London: Frank Cass, 1996.

Sulleiman, Ezna, and John Waterbury, "Analyzing Privatization in Industrial and Developing Countries." In *The Political Economy of Public Sector Reform and Privatization*, edited by Suleiman and Waterbury.

Boulder: Westview Press, 1990.

Sullivan, Denis J. "Bureaucratic politics in Development Assistance: The Failure of American Aid in Egypt." *Administration and Society* 23 (May 1991): 29-53.

Taber, John R. "Performance-Based Contracting: A Primer." USAID mimeo, 1996.

Tang, Kwong-leung. "Efficiency of the Private Sector: A Critical Review of Empirical Evidence from Public Services." *International Review of Administrative Sciences* 63 (December 1997): 459-474.

Tarnoff, Curt, and Larry Q. Nowels. *U.S. Foreign Assistance: The Rationale, The Record, and the Challenges in the Post-Cold War Era.* Washington, D.C.: National Planning Association, 1994.

Tendler, Judith. *Inside Foreign Aid.* Baltimore: Johns Hopkins University Press, 1975.

Treilbileock, Michael J. "Can Government be Reinvented?" In *The State Under Contract*, edited by Jonathan Boston, 1-35. Wellington, New Zealand: Briget Williams Books, 1995.

Tullock, Gordon. "Public Choice." *The New Palgrave Dictionary of Economics.* London: Macmillan Publishers, 1990: 1040-1044.

Tvedt, Terje. *Angels of Mercy or Development Diplomats?: NGOs and Foreign Aid.* London: Africa Press, 1998.

United Nations Development Program (UNDP). "Technical Cooperation in African Development: An Assessment of its Effectiveness in Support of the UN Program of Action for African Economic Recovery and Development, 1986-1990," UNPAAERD, UNDP, March 1989.

——. *Human Development Report 1996.* New York: United Nations Development Program and Oxford University Press, 1996.

U.S. Agency for International Development (USAID). *A Review of AID's Experience in Private Sector Development.* Washington, D.C.: AID Program Evaluation Report No. 14, Agency for International Development, 1985.

——. "USAID Procurement Reform: Memorandum for the Executive Staff from the Administrator," January 6, 1994.

——. "USAID Means Business." Washington, D.C., Center for Trade and Investment, US Agency for International Development, 1995a.

——. *Guide to Doing Business with the U.S. Agency for International Development.* Washington, D.C., 1995b

——. *Toward the New USAID: An NPR Progress Report.* Washington, D.C.: U.S. Agency for International Development, 1996

——. *Federal Acquisition Regulations.* Washington, D.C.: Office of Procurement, USAID, January 1996.

——. *U.S. Overseas Loans and Grants and Assistance from International*

Organizations, Obligations and Loan Authorizations July 1, 1945-September 30, 1995, Office of Budget, USAID, 1996.

——. *Congressional Presentation FY1997*. Summary Tables, 1996.

——. *Congressional Presentation FY1998*. Summary Tables, 1997.

——. *Guidance for Award Fee Contracting*. Office of Procurement, Policy Division, Contract Information Bulletin 97-12, 1997a.

——. *U.S. Agency for International Development Congressional Presentation for 1998*. Washington, D.C.: USAID, Washington, D.C., February 1997b.

——. *Guidelines for Conducting Past-Performance Evaluations*. Special Projects Unit, Office of Procurement, Washington, D.C., March 1997c.

——. "USAID Suspends Two Harvard Agreements in Russia." Washington, D.C.: USAID Press Office, January 1997d.

——. *Why Foreign Aid?* Washington, D.C., n.d.

——. *An Assessment of the State of the USAID/PVO Partnership*, Washington, D.C.: USAID Advisory Committee on Voluntary Foreign Aid, June 1997

——. *The USAID Fact Sheet*, Washington, D.C.: USAID Press Office, 1998

U.S. Congress. *Government Contract Mismanagement*. Hearing before the Subcommittee on Oversight and Investigations of the Committee on Energy and Commerce, House of Representatives, 102 Congress, Serial No. 102-166, Washington, D.C., 3 December, 1992.

U.S. Senate. *The Benefits of Foreign Aid to the United States Economy*. Hearing before a Subcommittee of the Committee on Appropriations of the U.S. Senate, 16 September, 1996.

Vellinga, Menno, ed. *The Changing Role of the State in Latin America*. Boulder: Westview Press, 1997.

von Opstal, Debra. *Road Map for Federal Acquisition (FAR) Reform: A Report of the CSIS Working Group*, Washington, D.C.: Center for Strategic and International Studies, 1995.

Wade, Robert. Governing the Market: Economic Theory and the Role of Government in Asian Industrialization. Princeton: Princeton University Press, 1990.

Wedel, Janine R. "The Harvard Boys Do Russia." *The Nation* 226, 1 June 1998a: 11-16.

——. *Collision and Collusion: The Strange Case of Western Aid to Eastern Europe*. New York: St. Martin's Press, 1998b.

Weisbrod, Robert A., ed. *To Profit or Not to Profit: The Commercial Transformation of the Nonprofit Sector.* Cambridge: Cambridge University Press, 1998.

White, Gordon. *The Macroeconomics of Foreign Aid*. Stockholm: SASDA, Ministry of Foreign Affairs, 1994.

——. "How Much Aid Is Used for Poverty Reduction?" *IDS Bulletin* 27, No 1 (1996): 83-99.

Williamson, O.E. "Transaction Cost Economics: The Governance of Contractual Relationships." *Journal of Law and Economics* 22 (October 1979): 233-262.

Winston, Clifford. "Economic Deregulation: Days of Reckoning for Microeconomists." *Journal of Economic Literature* 31 (September 1993): 1263-1289.

Wood, Robert E. *From Marshall Plan to Debt Crisis: Foreign Aid and Development Choices in the World Economy.* Berkeley: University of California Press, 1986.

——. "Rethinking Economic Aid." In *Foreign Aid Toward the Millenium*, edited by Steven Hook, 19-37. Boulder: Lynne Rienner Publishers, 1996.

Woods, Alan. *Development and the National Interest: U.S. Economic Assistance into the 21st Century.* Washington: Agency for International Development, February 1989.

World Bank. *World Development Report 1996*, Washington, D.C.: The World Bank, 1997.

York, Byron. "Big Al's Big Scam." *The American Spectator*, February 1996: 39-43.

Zimmerman, Robert F. *Dollars, Diplomacy and Dependency: The Dilemmas of Foreign Aid.* Boulder: Lynne Rienner Publishers, 1993.

Zimmerman, Robert F., and Steven W. Hook, "The Assault on U.S. Foreign Aid." In *Foreign Aid Toward the Millenium*, edited by Steven Hook, 57-73. Boulder: Lynne Rienner, 1996.

Index

About the Author

RUBÉN BERRÍOS teaches in the International MBA Program at Point Park College. He has many years of international development experience, particularly in Latin America and the Caribbean. He has published numerous book chapters and articles in professional journals on development and comparative economic issues. Most recently he was visiting research fellow at the Institute of Developing Economies in Tokyo.

ISBN 0-275-96633-X

9 780275 966331

90000>

EAN

HARDCOVER BAR CODE

DATE DUE			
		DEC 1 9 2007	
SEP 1 2 2000			
NOV 2 8 2000			
OCT 0 4 2002			
GAYLORD			PRINTED IN U.S.A.